PSALMS FOR

Praying

PSALMS FOR

Praying

An Invitation
to Wholeness

TENTH ANNIVERSARY EDITION

NAN C. MERRILL

continuum

NEW YORK • LONDON

2008

The Continuum International Publishing Group Inc
80 Maiden Lane, New York, NY 10038

The Continuum International Publishing Group Ltd
The Tower Building, 11 York Road, London SE1 7NX

Printed in the United States of America

Library of Congress Cataloging-in-Publication Data

Merrill, Nan C.
Psalms for praying : an invitation to wholeness /
Nan C. Merrill. — 10th anniversary ed.
p.   cm.
ISBN-13: 978-0-8264-1905-7 (hardcover : alk. paper)
ISBN-10: 0-8264-1905-4 (hardcover : alk. paper)
ISBN-13: 978-0-8264-1906-4 (pbk. : alk. paper)
ISBN-10: 0-8264-1906-2 (pbk. : alk. paper)
1. Bible. O.T. Psalms—Prayers.   I. Title.
BS1430.5.M47   2006
223'.205209—dc22   2006030718

Continuum Publishing is committed to preserving ancient forests
and natural resources. We have elected to print this title on 50%
postconsumer waste recycled paper. As a result, this book has saved:
41 trees
1,918 lbs of solid waste
14,937 gallons of water
29 million BTUs of total energy
3,598 pounds of greenhouse gases
Continuum is a member of Green Press Initiative, a nonprofit
program dedicated to supporting publishers in their efforts to
reduce their use of fiber obtained from endangered forests. For
more information, go to www.greenpressinitiative.org.

*Dedicated to
the indwelling Divine Guest
whose Voice is heard
in the Silence*

Preface to the Tenth Anniversary Edition

Out of the silence, as I continue to meditate and dialogue with the Psalms, they become living prayers that evoke, albeit subtly, new insights, new emphases, new words and phrases, and in some instances, new verses. This Tenth Anniversary Edition bears witness to the heightened consciousness that is reflected in the spiritual growth burgeoning in every arena of life. The plight of our world cries out for active, focused prayer.

Since the nations' governments, environment, and peoples of the world are repeatedly changing, we are all faced with new challenges; in response, prayers of millions of individuals are rising up to bear witness to Love in these unsettling times. Praying the Psalms with heartfelt attention and intention can be a step toward our souls awakening to the Love Consciousness being brought into the light out of the ashes of terror and destruction in our day.

To pray is to be transformed. We become One in the Silence with pray-ers from every country who are scattering seeds of love and light into the chaos; thus, we blanket the world with a web of peace.

Just as light dispels darkness, fear cannot exist where love abides. I pray that this Tenth Anniversary Edition will be as a beacon shining light and blessing into your prayer life. May the prayers of all who read, pray, or sing the Psalms help awaken us to the Peace of the Beloved indwelling in every soul. May we *become* peace, and may we each know the gentle joy of co-creating with the Beloved on behalf of Earth: our home.

In the Silence,
Nan Merrill

Preface

*W*ho among us has not yearned TO KNOW the Unknowable? For most, these moments are fleeting glimpses that may last a lifetime; in some, a Fire is kindled and life becomes a quest to live in Holy Surrender; and though fewer in number, saints dwell among us who know the Beloved, who aspire simply to co-create in harmony with the One, who is Love and Light and Power. To cherish the Beloved as you are cherished is to live in a mutual bonding that calls for action.

The Psalms have ever been a response to these deep yearnings: cries of the soul . . . songs of surrender . . . paeans of praise. The Psalms of the Hebrew Scripture often reflect a patriarchal society based on fear and guilt that projects evil and sin onto outer enemies. *Psalms for Praying* reflects the reciprocity of Divine Love that opens the heart to forgiveness, reconciliation, and healing. Affirming the life-giving fruits of love and acknowledging the isolation and loneliness of those separated from Love, may serve to awaken the heart to move toward wholeness and holiness.

Aspiring to live in a spirit of cooperation, co-creation, and companionship with the Beloved, rather than invoking a spirit of competition with God, other individuals and nations—so much a part of the Hebrew Scripture Psalms—seems clearly a more loving movement toward engendering peace, harmony, and healing in our wounded world.

Yet, let it be understood that *Psalms for Praying: An Invitation to Wholeness* is in no way meant to replace the well-loved, still meaningful, and historically important Psalms of the Hebrew Scripture. May it stand as a companion, a dialogue, if you will, of one age speaking with a later age. May it serve as an invitation to listen to the Voice of Silence that speaks within your own soul.

N.M.

Psalm 1

*B*lessed are those
    who walk hand in hand
        with goodness,
    who stand beside virtue,
    who sit in the seat of truth;
For their delight is in the Spirit of Love,
    and in Love's heart they dwell
        day and night.
They are like trees planted by
        streams of water,
    that yield fruit in due season,
    and their leaves flourish;
And in all that they do, they give life.
The unloving are not so;
    they are like dandelions which
        the wind blows away.
Turning from the Heart of Love
    they will know suffering and pain.
They will be isolated from wisdom;
    for Love knows the way of truth,
    the way of ignorance will perish
    as Love's penetrating Light
        breaks through hearts
            filled with illusions:
        forgiveness is the way.

Psalm 2

Why do nations and people plot against
            one another,
    setting themselves apart and conspiring
        against the Beloved and those
        who follow Love's way?
They say to themselves, "We are free
        of Love's law;
      humility and service are for others."

The Beloved, who is ever present, can but
        smile at their foolishness,
      knowing that one day, they will
        fall to their knees in regret.
Distracted by greed and arrogance
      they do not hear the Beloved's Voice
        whispering in the silence:
"Awaken all of you living in darkness!
We are all One in Love Consciousness.
      You live in my Heart even as
        I dwell in yours.

For you are mine; I am your Beloved.
      I have given you abundant life
        to love and care for all Creation.
      May it be for the delight of All.
Yet, to know Me, fears and illusions
        must be faced,
      as an iron rod hitting a clay pot
      shining Light into the darkness."

Blessed are all who have asked
                    for forgiveness,
        whose hearts radiate the Love
        we all are at the core.

Psalm 3

O Beloved, how numerous are my fears!
        They rise up within me whispering
                there is no help for you.

Yet You, O Beloved, radiate Love
                around me, my glory;
        gratitude becomes my song,
When I cry out to You,
        You answer within my heart.

I lie down to sleep; if I should
        awaken, my Beloved is there
                holding me with strength
                        and tenderness.
                I feel secure.
Now, I shall forgive all illusions
        that my ego tries to build.
For my courage is in You, O Love,
You who are the Lover hidden
        in every heart.

Rise up, Love! Set me free!
    For through your guidance,
    my fears will fade into love.
Free from fear, I will know
    the Oneness of Being that
        encompasses Everything!
I shall be free to serve Love
    with a glad and open heart.

Psalm 4

Answer me when I call, O Beloved of my heart!
    You enveloped me in Love when I was
        in dire distress.
Be gracious to me now; hear my prayer!

O friends, how long will my reputation
        suffer shame?
How long will you listen to false words?
    I seek only what is life-giving.

You know that the Beloved dwells with all
      who are filled with love;
    Love hears when our hearts cry out.
Though you may feel angry,
        do not give in to fear;
Commune with the Heart of your heart
      as you rest; be in silence.
      Bask in the stillness.

Face your fears with forgiveness,
and trust in Love.

There are many who say,
"Grant us special favors,
O Mighty One!
Bestow upon us your grace that
we may prosper!"
Love has brought more joy to my heart
than they have when their banks
are filled.
In peace will I spend my days and
sleep at night;
For You alone, my Beloved,
teach me the way of Love!

Psalm 5

Give ear to my words, O my Beloved;
give heed to my groaning.
Listen to the sound of my cry,
my Love, Heart of my heart,
for to You do I pray.
O my Beloved, in the morning
You hear my voice;
throughout the day, I offer myself to You;
I wait for You in silence.
For You are love and You delight
in goodness;
all that is of love walks with You.

The humble stand before You;
>You dwell with those who open
>>their hearts to receive You.
You smile on those who speak truth;
>tears from your Heart fall on those
>>who separate themselves from You.

Through the abundance of your steadfast love
>I shall enter your house;
I shall worship in your holy temple
>with reverence for You.

Lead me, O my Beloved, in your mercy
>lighten my fears;
>make your way straight before me
>that I may follow.
For there is no truth in fear;
>it leads to separation,
>it opens the door to loneliness,
>it speaks not with integrity,
>>but out of illusion;
Let this guilt I bear, my Beloved,
>be seen in your light;
>forgive the many false ways I have,
>>surround them with your love,
>for they keep me separated from You.

Let all who come to Love rejoice,
>let them sing for joy!
And protect them, so that those
>who live in your love may
>dance in your light.
For You bless the peaceful and just,
>O Friend to all,
You encircle them with your healing light
>and hold them in your love.

Psalm 6

O my Beloved, though I have turned from You,
     continue to enfold me with your love;
Be gracious to me, Heart of my heart,
     for I am sad and weary.
Surround me with your healing Light,
     that my body, mind, and soul might heal.
How long must I wait, O Love?

I open the door of my heart to You,
          my Beloved,
Enter in and imbue me with your steadfast Love.
I shall remember You all my days;
I shall sing praises to You throughout the
          nights.

I am tired of so many fears;
I cry myself to sleep at night, while
     grief and feelings of guilt
          bedim my eyes with tears.
All my doubts, my fears, are creating walls
          so that I know not love.

Depart from me,
     you enemies of wholeness,
     for the Beloved is aware of my cry;
Love has heard my prayer,
     and hastens to answer my call.
Though my fears are running for cover,
     yet they shall be forgiven
          by Love;
Illusions that lived in the ego
     can now turn to the Light:
          I will know peace as I
               return Home.

Psalm 7

O my Beloved, to You do I draw close;
    when all my inner fears well up,
    enfold me in your strong arms;
    otherwise, like a fiery dragon,
        my fears will consume me,
        I shall live in my illusions.

O Love, if I have been unkind, unloving
    or acted in ignorance,
    if I have been unjust to others
        seeing my own weaknesses in them,
Forgive me, O Gracious One,
    and give me the grace to make amends,
    that we may walk again in harmony.

Arise, O Beloved, in your steadfast love,
    shield me from the demons within;
Stay near me, Heart of my heart, and
    I shall be strong to face
        my fears and illusions.
Let all the fragmented parts of my being
        gather around You,
    help me to face them one by one.
Love's healing presence will mend
    all that has been broken;
    I shall once again be made whole.

O let the terrible fears that keep me
    from loving come to an end!
Establish integrity within me,
    You who readily forgive us,
    You who call us back Home to love.

My shield is with Love,
>who dwells within my open heart.
Love is kind and gracious,
>quick to forgive and pleased
>>to share
>the great Mystery of life!

If I close my heart to Love,
>the Beloved awaits close by;
Love cultivates the soil of my heart,
>planting sacred seeds in its garden.
Take notice! Even should I wander
>far from Love's path,
>though I err and walk on roads
>>of illusion and darkness,
>should I act out of fear and
>>ignorance,
>falling into a pit of despair,
Yet will Love remain constant and sure.
I shall dwell with Love in gratitude
>and joy;
I shall sing praises to the Beloved,
>knowing my Oneness with All.

Psalm 8

O Love, my Beloved,
How powerful is your Name
>in all the earth!
You, whose glory is sung in heaven
>by the angels and saints,

Who with the innocence and
                    spontaneity of a child,
Confound those who are mighty
                    and proud,
You comfort the unloving and fearful.

When I look up at the heavens,
        at the work of Love's creation,
        at the infinite variety of your Plan,
What is woman that You rejoice in her,
And man that You do delight in him?
        You have made us in your image,
        You fill us with your Love;
You have made us co-creators of
                    the earth!
        guardians of the planet!
        to care for all your creatures,
        to tend the land, the sea,
                    and the air we breathe;
        all that You have made,
                    You have placed in our hands.

O Love, my Beloved,
How powerful is your Name
            in all the earth!

Psalm 9

Give thanks to the Beloved
    with your whole heart;
      tell the story of Love's way;
Be glad and dance with joy;
Sing praises to the Name above
        all names,
    as illusions are dispelled,
    as they fade away before
        Love's face.
For You, O Beloved, are ever-present,
    ready to be known in open hearts.

You know each nation, and see
      how they destroy one another;
    chaos and darkness rise up
        blind to Love's way;
    forgotten is creation's glory,
    false power seeks to destroy
        The Divine Plan.
Yet Love will abide forever; for
You have established yourself
      in secret places
    seeking out receptive hearts,
    ready to enter and make your
        dwelling place within.

Love is a stronghold for the oppressed,
    a foundation in difficult times.
And those who know Love's Name
    therein place their trust.
For You, O Beloved, are ever-present
    to those who know You.

Sing praises to the One, who is Love,
who dwells in your heart!
Tell everyone of Love's wonder-
filled deeds!
For those who know compassion
will remember those in need.

Be gracious to me, O Beloved!
Behold what I suffer out of fear,
O You, who awakened me from
a living death,
I sing of your glory,
from the depths of my being,
I rejoice and give thanks for
your faithful love.

The nations are sinking into a pit
of their own making;
into the web which they are weaving,
will they be caught.
Love will make Itself known
with a strength stronger than
ten thousand armies!
The unloving will have to face
themselves,
all nations that are unjust.
For the oppressed will be released,
And the hope of the poor will
be realized.

Arise, O Love! Have your way with us;
let the nations bow before You
and ask forgiveness!
Let your healing Light stream forth,
O Love,
Let the nations commit themselves
to your Plan!

Psalm 10

Why do You seem so far from me,
        O Silent One?
Where do You hide when fears
            beset me?
I boast and strike out against
        those weaker than myself,
        even knowing I shall be caught in
            a snare of my own making.

When I feel insecure,
        I look for pleasure,
        greed grips my heart and I
            banish You from my life.
In my pride, I seek You not,
I come to believe, "I am the Creator
        of my world."

I even prosper at times:
        your Love seems too great for me,
            out of my reach;
        as for my fears, I pretend they
            do not exist.
I think in my heart, "I do not need
            You;
        adversity will come only to others."

My eyes watch carefully for another's
            weakness,
I wait in secret like a spider
            in its web;
I wait that I might seize those who
            are weaker than myself,
        draw others into my web,
        that I might use them to
            feel powerful.

Like me, the fearful are crushed,
     we fall by our own illusions.
Then we think in our hearts,
          "I do not deserve Love;
          my Beloved has forgotten me,
          I am alone with my fears forever."

Awaken, O Love! O You who created me,
               return to my side;
          forget me not in my weakness.
Why do I turn my back to You,
          and say in my heart, "You will
               not take notice of me?"
You do see me. Yes, You know
               my anguish and fears;
          You make yourself known to me
When I commit myself into your hands.
You are ever my strength and comforter.

Help me to break the webs
               I have woven,
To seek out and forgive my illusions
          until You find not one.
For You are my Beloved forever;
          All that is separate from You
               will disappear through Love.

O my Beloved, You hear my heart;
          strengthen me and answer
               my soul's Cry!
May I live with integrity, as
          a loving presence in the world.
May my will be one with your Will!

Psalm 11

In the Beloved do I make my retreat.
       How can you say to me,
        "Flee like a bird to the
               mountains;
        for lo, the unloving bend the bow,
        fitting their arrow to the string;
        they aim to destroy what is good?"
If the foundations of goodness are
               undermined, what will remain?

The Beloved dwells in the Holy Temple,
        the sacred altar within our hearts,
        loving and testing each one of us.
Divine Love offers both the good
        and the unloving opportunities
        to grow, to become whole,
        enduring with Love those who
               choose the way of darkness.

Those who walk in the ego's illusions
        will live with fear and doubt;
        ignorance will be their guide.
For our Creator is just, gifting us
               with free will;
Those who walk in the Light
        will behold the Beloved's face
               in everyone they meet.

Psalm 12

Come to our aid, O Beloved!
      darkness seems to pervade the earth;
Where is the faith, the integrity
      that once lived in the hearts
         of your people?
Where is the truth, the trust
      that made its home in us?

O Love, cleanse us from our double talk,
Create in us new and single hearts,
Spare us from those who think,
      "Our speeches will win over all.
         Words are our weapons;
         no one can master us!"

"For the hearts of those who call to Me,
For those who cry out for wholeness,
      I shall make Myself known,"
      says the Beloved;
"I shall make Myself known in their
      hearts."

The promises of Love are pure,
      like silver refined in a crucible,
      like gold purified seven times.
Be our safeguard, O Blessed One,
Stay close by throughout these dark days
      where unloving hearts seem to abound.
Come to our aid, O Beloved!

Psalm 13

How long, my Beloved?
        Will you forget me forever?
How long will you hide your
                face from me?
How long must I bear this pain
                in my soul,
        and live with sorrow
                all the day?
How long will fear rule my life?

Notice my heart and answer me,
                O my Beloved;
        enlighten me, lest I walk as
                one dead to life;
Lest my ego fears say,
        "We have won the day;"
Lest they rejoice in their strength.

As I trust in your steadfast
                Love;
        my heart will rejoice,
                for in You is freedom.
I shall sing to the Beloved,
        who has answered my prayers
                a thousand fold!
Come, O Beloved, make your home
        in my heart.

Psalm 14

The hearts of fools say,
    "There is no power in Love."
They live in illusion; they torture
        themselves and others;
They walk alone in utter darkness
        calling it light.

Love looks into the heart
        of every person,
    to see if any act with wisdom,
    if any seek to walk with Love.
Many there are who have gone
        astray,
    who are ruled by greed and power.
Is there one who is wise and kind?

Have they no knowledge,
        all the ignorant,
    who devour people and nations
        as if they were bread,
    and never call upon Love?
One day terror will reign in their hearts;
    for Love's friend is Truth
    and in Truth will those
        who seek Love's way
        be set free.

O that the hearts of all Love's
        children
    might call upon their angels!

O that all people, all nations
    might know that harmony
    and beauty reside in diversity,
    that we are all One in
        Love Consciousness!
O that we may rejoice in Life
    in the abundance of Love's gifts
    created and given to all!

Psalm 15

O Beloved, You invite us to rest
    in the abode of your Heart,
        to forgive our weaknesses
            and renew our love.
Who will respond with hearts
    opened wide to Love?

Those who walk with integrity, who
    are in harmony with your Word,
        and sing the heart's song;
Whose tongues speak truth
    judging not others and
    seeking only the good;
Whose eyes behold not the outer
        garments of the body,
    but see within the inner robe
        of Love;

Whose own weaknesses are acknowledged
and brought to light in prayer;
Those who are just in all affairs of life
and take not advantage
of another.

Those who dwell in the Heart of Love,
who act justly, with integrity,
will join the Dance of Life,
will sing the Songs of Joy!
Their family, friends and, indeed,
the world
will be blessed by their love.

Psalm 16

Remain ever before me,
O Living Presence,
for in You am I safe.
You are my Beloved; in You
and through You
I can do all things.

I look to those who are at one
with You and learn
from them of your ways;
My delight increases each time
I sense your Presence
within me!

Songs of praise well up from
my heart!

Love is my chosen food, my cup,
holding me in its power.
Where I have come from,
Where'er I shall go,
Love is my birthright,
my true estate.

I bless the Counselor who guides
my way;
in the night also does my heart
instruct me.
I walk beside the Spirit of Truth;
I celebrate the Light.
I bask in The Oneness of All!
Thus my heart is glad, and my soul
rejoices;
I shall not be afraid,
nor fall into the pit of despair;
For in Love's presence I know fullness
of joy.

You are my Beloved and, in You
will I live forever!

Psalm 17

Listen to my heart, O Love Divine;
    hear the cry within me!
Heed my prayer from lips that
    would utter truth!
For in You do I seek justice!
Be Thou my eyes that I may
    see with clarity.

If You try my heart,
    if You visit me by night,
    if You test me, You will
        discover
    My only desire is to
    draw closer to You.
I see the injustice and the
        oppression
    piercing the hearts of your people.

Be Thou my feet that I may walk
    along your paths;
    that I may be a benevolent
    presence on life's highway.

I call upon You knowing You will
    answer me,
    Heart of my heart;
    incline your ear to me,
    hear my words.
Wondrously show your steadfast love,
O Love Divine, You walk beside me
    giving me strength to face
    the fears that dwell within.

Keep me as the apple of your eye;
　　hide me in the shadow of your
　　　　wings,
　　from all that would separate me
　　　　from your Love.

Open my heart that compassion may
　　　　be my companion;
Where I meet pride, humble me;
Where I meet anger, calm my fears;
Where I meet injustice, cause me
　　to act in love's way.
May I be as gentle as the doe,
　　as fearless as the lion,
　　as faithful as the dog.

Arise, O Heart of Love!
　　confront all within me
　　that is not whole!

Deliver me from deadly fears
　　　　and doubts, shine
　　your Light into my darkness.
May my heart receive the bounty of
　　　　your Love,
May my children and their children
　　walk with You in gratitude
　　　　and joy.

For I shall behold your face
　　　　in Truth,
　　when I am fully awake,
I shall dwell in the house of
　　love and peace and joy!

Psalm 18

I abandon myself to You,
    O Living Presence, my strength.
You are my stronghold,
    my freedom,
    Almighty One, the rock and
        foundation of my life,
    Just One, tower of strength,
        the source of truth and light,
I call upon You, Heart of my heart,
        singing praises to your Name,
    and fear no longer holds me.

The demons of darkness assailed me,
    the blindness of ignorance led me
        astray;
The shadows of fear paralyzed me,
    the anguish of loneliness
        confronted me.
In my distress I called out to You,
    O Gracious One;
    to You I cried for help.
You heard my voice, O Loving Presence,
    You hearkened to my cry.

Then did You, O Divine Presence, show
        unto me a vision:
    the earth reeled and rocked;
The foundations of the mountains
    trembled and quaked,
As if to slough off the ravages
        of destruction
    perpetrated by greedy hands.

On the wings of the wind, You did come,
with darkness a covering
around You,
a canopy of thick clouds
dark with water.
Out of the brightness before You
there broke through the clouds
hailstones,
coals of fire lept from
the mountaintops.
As your voice uttered in the heavens,
thunder and lightning stormed
the earth;
like arrows from a bow,
the peoples scattered.

Yet there was no safe haven,
no hiding place from fear.
Then the channels of the sea were seen,
and the foundations of the world
laid bare,
The earth gave a mighty shudder
then settled down to heal in
the Silence.

O Compassionate One, You reached
from on high, You took me,
You drew me out of many waters.
You delivered me from the fears
that bound me, and
from ignorance that blinded me;
for they threatened to overcome me,
to separate me from You.

They came upon me when I looked not
            to You;
        yet You, O Merciful One, were
            ever present.
You brought me forth into the Light;
You released my fears, You delighted
            in me.

O Holy One, You see the intentions
            of my heart;
        As I surrender to your love,
            I grow in peace and gratitude.
For to lose my life is to find Life;
        O keep me steadfast in my love
            for You, Life of my life!
The spirit of your Word is ever
            before me,
        the Counselor ever present to
            guide me.
I pray for a clean heart, O Beloved,
            to be free from guilt.
May I walk with You justly, with mercy
            and in peace,
        a mirror of your Love in the world.

Those who love truth will see your Light;
Those who walk in justice, will see
            your Mercy;
Those who live with integrity, will see
            You in all they meet;
But those whose path is crooked,
        who walk on the low road,
            will live in the shadows of fear.

The humble are always close to You,
the haughty, too distracted
to see,
will one day fall.

Yes, You are the Light of my life;
You shine through my darkness.
Yes, with You I can do all things;
and my spirit soars like
an eagle.
Your ways lead to wholeness,
O Loving Presence;
Your Word in me is life;
How tenderly You live in my heart!

For who is our Creator, but
the source of Love!
And who is Life, except
the Divine Presence!—
You, who gird me with strength,
and lead me in the way
of Truth.
You make my feet like hinds' feet,
and set me secure on the heights.
You teach me the way of justice,
that I might speak out against
oppression.
You give me a hunger for silence,
that I might know the power
of prayer,
and You support me in solitude.
You give me freedom to choose the
journey road;
I elect the narrow way.

For I pursued my fears and faced them
      and did not run back until
         I was free.
I saw each one through, so that they
        were not able to rise;
      they were transformed by Love.
For You enabled me with strength
        to look deep within;
      holding me when fears threatened
      to overwhelm me.

You brought forgiveness into the
        darkness,
      and softened my heart to forgive
      my adversaries.
Though my fears rose up, as old friends
        being betrayed,
      Love brought them down.
What had been weakness and weeds,
      now turned to strength and roses;
        yes, my fears were redeemed by Love.
You delivered me from prejudice and
        intolerance;
      You opened my heart to all nations;
      people whom I had not known
      befriended me.
As soon as they beheld the radiance
      of your Love,
      they came to my door;
      strangers came desiring to
      hear your Word.
Yes, strangers came—and those who had
      separated themselves from Love,
      they came seeking release from
      their fears.

The Most High lives; blessed be
        my Rock,
    and exalted be the Heart of
        my heart,
The Loving One, who helped me face
        my fears
    and opened my heart to the poor;
You delivered me out of the darkness
        of ignorance;
    Yes, You did bring victory over
        my illusions,
    You led me into harmony and
        wholeness.

For this I will extol You, O my Beloved,
        among the nations,
    and sing praises to your Name.
Peace, gratitude, love, and assurance are
        gifts bestowed by Love.
    May all peoples live in your Truth
        in the unity of peace forever.
        Amen.

Psalm 19

The heavens declare the glory
        of the Creator;
    the firmament proclaims the
        handiwork of Love.

Day to day speech pours forth
        and night to night knowledge
            is revealed.
There is no speech,
        nor are there words;
        their voice is not heard;
Yet does their music resound
            through all the earth,
        and their words echo to
            the ends of the world.

In them a tent for the sun is set,
        which is like a bride and groom
            on their wedding night
        as they sing love's song and
            celebrate the dance of life.
Its rising is in eternity,
        and its circuit to infinity;
Nothing is hidden from
        the sunlight.

The law of Love is perfect,
        reviving the soul;
The testimony of Love is sure,
        making wise the simple;
The precepts of Love are right,
        rejoicing the heart;
The authority of Love is pure,
        enlightening the eyes;
The spirit of Love is glorious,
        enduring forever;
The rites of Love are true,
        awakening compassion.

More to be desired are they
            than gold,
        even much fine gold;

Sweeter also than honey and
    drippings of the honeycomb.
Moreover, by them are the loving
            guided;
        in keeping them there is
            great reward.

But who can discern their own
            weaknesses?
        Cleanse me, O Love, from
            all my hidden faults.
Keep me from boldly acting in
            error; let my fears
        and illusions not have dominion
            over me!
Then shall I become a beneficial
            presence,
        freely and fully surrendered
            to your Love.

Let the words of my mouth
        and the meditation of my heart
        find favor in your Heart
O my Beloved, my strength and
            my joy!

Psalm 20

May the Great Birther who created
    you in wholeness, comfort you
        when you call!
May the Name of Love be your
        protection
    and rise up in your heart
        as a tower of strength!
May all you have given in gratitude
        and with open hands
    be returned to you a hundredfold!
May your heart's desires and all of
        Love's plans for you
    be fulfilled in due season!
Let us shout for joy as Love
        triumphs over fear;
Let our thankful hearts sing in
    loud acclamation to the
        Beloved, who answers
    our heartfelt prayers for
        well-being.

Now I know that Love comes to all
    who open their hearts, and
        dwells therein
    offering gifts of peace and
        harmony.
Some may boast of wealth and
        personal power;
    they will stumble and fall.
Let us boast of the One who
    comes in the Name of Love;
We shall rise up strong and sure.

O Beloved, You who created us,
You bless us with your Love,
For you are the Divine Guest
dwelling within our hearts.

Psalm 21

In your strength I rejoice,
O my Beloved,
and in your Presence
my heart finds rest!
You heed the heart's desire,
answering the cry of the soul,
and You bestow blessing upon
blessing;
Your Love is as a crown of fine
gold upon my head.
I asked for life; and life
you did provide,
eternal life comes through
your Love.
All glory be yours, O Loving Presence,
splendor and majesty are
your raiment.
Yes, your blessings are forever;
You delight me with the joy
of your Presence.

Forever I will put my trust in You;
  and as I abandon myself to You
   in love,
  I am assured of peace.

You root out my fears; standing
  firm beside me as I face
   the shadows within.
Like a blazing sun your light shines.
My fears flee from your sight;
  your fire consumes them.
Generations to come will sing to
   your glory
In gratitude and joy for creation's
   bountiful gifts of life.
For You put fears to flight, that
  love and justice might reign.

All praise be yours, O Wondrous One!
  Forever will I be grateful
   and give witness to your
   peace and love that frees us.

Psalm 22

O my Beloved, why have You
  forsaken me?
Why are You so far, abandoning me
  as I groan in misery?

O my Beloved, I cry by day, but
            You do not answer;
        and by night, but find no rest.

Yet You are holy, praised
            through all generations.
In You our parents trusted;
        they trusted, and You did come
            to their aid.
To You they cried, and were heard;
        in You they trusted, and
            were not disappointed.

But I seem as nothing, hardly alive;
        scorned and despised by many.
Those who see me make fun
            at my expense,
        they ridicule and gossip
            among themselves;
"Commit yourself to the Most High;
        let Love deliver you,
        you who delight in the Most High!"

Yet, You are the One who took me
            from the womb;
        You kept me safe upon my
            mother's breasts.
Upon You I was cast from my birth,
        and ever since my mother bore me,
            You have been my strength.
Come close to me, for trouble is near
        and there is none to help.

Many, like bulls, surround me,
        they come at me with great force.

With fire in their eyes
          and bellowing roars,
     they charge at me.

I am poured out like water,
          and all my bones are weak;
     my heart is like wax,
               melting within my breast;
My strength is broken as a
               shard of pottery,
          and my mouth is dry;
     You have laid me in the dust
               of death.

Yes, boars are round about me;
          a company of evildoers encircle me;
          they have pierced my hands and feet—
I can count all my bones—
          they stare and gloat over me
          awaiting my demise;
They divide my belongings among
               them,
          avariciously casting lots.

But You, O Beloved, be not far off!
          You, who are my help, hasten to
               my aid!
Free my soul from this agony,
          my life from the power of
               the boar!
Save me from the mouth of
               the lion,
          my afflicted soul from the
               horns of the bull!

I will tell of your Name to
          all I meet,
     in the midst of assemblies
          I will praise You;
You, who are in wonder of the Mystery,
          give praise!
For our loving Creator does not turn
          away from the afflicted,
And does not hide from them;
But their cries are heard,
          their prayers rise up to heaven.

To You, O Beloved, I lift up my voice
          in the great congregation;
     for You promise to remain with
          those whose love is steadfast.
The hungry shall eat and be
          satisfied;
Those who seek You shall sing praises!
Your Heart is our dwelling place forever!

All the ends of the earth shall
          remember
     and turn to Love's way;
And all the families of the nations
          shall bow down with grateful
          hearts.
For power and authority belong to
          the Most High,
     who rules over the nations.

Yes, the proud of the earth shall be
          humbled, while
     those who still live in fear
          and illusions will

separate themselves not knowing
the indwelling Peace of the Beloved.
Posterity shall know and serve Love,
telling of the One who abides in all
to the coming generations,
And proclaiming deliverance to a
people yet unborn
that the Most High dwells among us.

Psalm 23

O my Beloved, You are my shepherd,
I shall not want;
You bring me to green pastures
for rest
and lead me beside still waters
renewing my spirit;
You restore my soul.
You lead me in the path of
goodness
to follow Love's way.

Even though I walk through the
valley of the shadow and
of death,
I am not afraid;
For You are ever with me;
your rod and your staff
they guide me,

they give me strength
and comfort.

You prepare a table before me
in the presence of all my fears;
you bless me with oil,
my cup overflows.
Surely goodness and mercy will
follow me
all the days of my life;
and I shall dwell in the heart
of the Beloved forever.
Amen.

Psalm 24

The earth is yours, O Giver of Life,
in all its fulness and glory,
the world and all those who
dwell therein;
For You have founded it upon
the seas,
and established it upon
the rivers.

Who shall ascend your hill,
O Gracious One?
and who shall stand in your
holy place?

All who have clean hands and
             pure hearts,
        who do not lift up their souls
             to what is false,
        nor make vows deceitfully.
All these will be blessed by the
             Heart of Love,
        and renewed through forgiveness.
Such is the promise to those
        who seek Love's face.

Lift up your heads, O gates!
        and be lifted up,
             O ancient doors!
        that the Compassionate One
             may come in.
Who is the Compassionate One?
        The Beloved, strong and steadfast,
        the Beloved, firm and sure!
Lift up your heads, O gates!
        and be lifted up,
             O ancient doors!
        that the Compassionate One
             may come in!
Who is this Compassionate One?
        The Beloved, Heart of your heart,
             Life of your life,
        this is the Compassionate One!

Psalm 25

To You, O Love, I lift up my soul!
O Heart within my heart,
      in You I place my trust.
      Let me not feel unworthy;
      let not fear rule over me.
Yes! May all who open their hearts
      savor You and bless the earth!

Compel me to know your ways, O Love;
      instruct me upon your paths.
Lead me in your truth,
        and teach me,
      for through You will I know
        wholeness;
I shall reflect your Light
      both day and night.

I know of your mercy, Blessed One,
      and of your unconditional Love;
      You have been with me
        from the beginning.
Forgive the many times I have walked
      away from You
      choosing to follow my own will.
I seek your guidance, once again,
      I yearn to know your Peace.
Companion me as I open to your Will!

You are gracious and just,
        O Spirit of Truth,
      happy to guide those who
        miss their way;

You enjoy teaching all who are open,
    all who choose to live in truth.
Your paths are loving and sure,
      O Holy One, and
      those who give witness to You
      through their lives
    are blessed beyond measure.

Yet, all too often glorious gifts
    of Grace, of Love and Light,
      are veiled by my busyness.
I bow down before You;
    instruct me, that I might choose
      the way of love and truth.
I would live in your abundant Love,
    and my children as well.
Your friendship is offered to all
    whose hearts are open;
    You make known your promises
    to them.
My eyes are ever on You, Beloved,
    keep my feet from stumbling
    along the way.

Turn to me, O Holy One, and envelop me
    with your love, for
I am lonely and oppressed.
Relieve the blocks in my heart
    that keep me separated from You;
See all the darkness within me;
    fill it with your healing Light.
Look at my pain and all my fears;
    they shut out love and life.

Protect me and free me;
    let me not live as unworthy,
    for I would return Home to You.

May integrity and wholeness fill me
        as I dwell with You,
                O Loving Presence.

May we, together with the angels
        and the company of heaven,
        help unfold your Plan
                for planet Earth.

Psalm 26

Speak on my behalf, O Beloved,
        for I would choose the path
                that leads back Home,
        trusting in your love
                        without reserve.
        May my heart be as your Heart;
        May my mind be as your Mind.
May your steadfast love guide me
As I live according to your Will,
You, O Counselor, are my strength
        and my guide; so
I choose the path of peace
        and wholeness.

I walk with friends of integrity,
        and associate with those
                who live in truth;

I love the company of faith-filled
people,
and count myself among those
who make your Word their own.

Cleanse my heart in innocence
that I might childlike be,
Singing songs of thanksgiving
and proclaiming the
Beloved's way.

O Loving Presence, I cherish your
dwelling place, my heart;
O, that I might radiate Love Divine.
Keep me always in your presence,
Ever-ready to praise your Name.
Make me holy, complete in You,
Write my name among the saints.

For I choose the path of peace
and wholeness;
The Counselor is my strength
and my guide.
Standing with equanimity in heaven's
blessed company,
I shall know Love and Peace
beyond the world's understanding.
Blessed are You, O my Beloved!

Psalm 27

Love is my light and
               my salvation,
       whom shall I fear?
Love is the strength of
       my life,
Of whom shall I be afraid?

When fears assail me,
       rising up to accuse me,
Each one in turn shall be seen
       in Love's light.
Though a multitude of demons
               rise up within me,
       my heart shall not fear.
Though doubts and guilt do battle,
       yet shall I remain confident.

One thing have I asked of Love,
       that I shall ever seek:
That I might dwell in the
               Heart of Love
       all the days of my life,
To behold the Beauty of my Beloved,
       and to know Love's Plan.

For I shall hide in Love's heart
       in the day of trouble,
As in a tent in the desert,
Away from the noise of my fears.
And I shall rise above
       my struggles, my pain,
Shouting blessings of gratitude
       in Love's Heart

And singing melodies of praise
to my Beloved.

Hear, O my Beloved,
when I cry aloud,
be gracious and answer me!
You have said, "Seek my face."
My heart responds,
"Your face, my Beloved, do I seek;
hide not your face from me."

Do not turn from me,
You who have been my refuge.
Enfold me in your strong arms,
O Blessed One.
Though my father and mother
may not understand me,
You, my Beloved, know me and love me.

Teach me to be love,
as You are Love;
Lead me through each fear;
Hold my hand as I walk through
valleys of illusion each day,
That I may know your Peace.

I believe that I shall know the
Realm of Heaven,
of Love, here on Earth!

Call upon the Beloved,
be strong and trust
in the heart's courage.
Trust in the power of Love;
the Beloved's unconditional and
everlasting love for you.

Psalm 28

Heart of my heart, I call to You;
You hear my cry and support me.
Should You remain silent in me,
I walk as in a desert waste.
You heed the voice of my humble request
    when I call your holy Name,
    when I lift my hands,
        O Holy One,
    to acknowledge your power and glory.

Protect me from those who love
        You not,
    those who delight in their own law,
Whose words become meaningless
    by the deeds of their hearts.
In your justice, they will reap
    a harvest of loneliness;
In your mercy, they will receive
    a reward worthy of their acts.
For they, who remain separated
    from your love, O Beloved,
Will miss the joy of your blessed
    grace, the peace of your
        companioning Presence.

Blessed are You, Heart of my heart!
    for You heed the cry of my spirit.
You are my strength and my protection;
    into your hands I commend my soul.
My heart leaps as You come to my aid,
        and my lament becomes
    a song of exultation,
    a shout of praise to You,
        O my Comforter!

Remember well, O my friends,
The Spirit of Truth becomes known
       to all who are receptive to Love,
              giving strength and shelter.
Mercy and justice are our birthright—
Let us call on the Giver of Life
       to guide our feet into the
              way of peace, and
       to live in our hearts forever.
Blessed be the Name of the Most High!

Psalm 29

Give praise to the Beloved,
       O heavenly hosts,
Sing of Love's glory and strength.
Exalt the glory of Love's Name;
Adore the Beloved in holy splendor.

The voice of the Beloved is upon
              the waters;
Love's voice echoes over the oceans
              and seas.
The voice of Love is powerful,
       majestic is the heart of Love.

The mercy of the Beloved breaks the
              bonds of oppression,
       shatters the chains of injustice.

Love invites all to the dance of freedom,
     to sing the Beloved's song of truth.

The voice of Love strikes with fire
         upon hearts of stone.
The voice of Love uproots the thorns
         of fear,
      Love uproots fear in every open
         heart.

The voice of Love is heard in every storm,
     and strips the ego bare;
And in the heart's chapel, all cry,
     "Peace and Glory forever!"

The Beloved lives in our hearts;
     Love dwells with us forever.
You who awaken to the Light
        of universal Oneness
     will know the blessed joy
     of serving in the great Work
        of Love.

Psalm 30

All praise to You, O Beloved,
     for You have raised me up,
     and have not let my fears
       overwhelm me.

O Compassionate One, I cried
            for help, and You
            comforted me.
You, O Love, helped me release
        my soul from despair;
You gave me strength to face
            my fears; now
        love is awakening in me.

Sing praises to the Beloved,
            All you saints,
        giving thanks to Love's holy Name.
Love withdraws when we close our hearts,
        yet ever awaits an open door.
In the evening we may weep,
        yet joy comes with the morning.

In my prosperity, I had lost sight
            of Love,
        I found power in my wealth.
In your mercy, O Beloved, my foundations
            You shook,
        and in recognizing my separation
            from You,
        I was dismayed.

I cried to You for help; to You,
        I pleaded for forgiveness:
                "What profit in my riches if
                I am separated from Love?
                Will emptiness praise You?
Will it tell of your faithfulness?
Hear me, O Beloved, and be gracious to me!
        O Love, hasten to my assistance!"

And You turned my mourning into dancing;
    You set me free and
        clothed me with gladness.
My soul rejoices and is glad in You;
    songs of gratitude fill My soul
        rising up to You, O Beloved.
        Amen.

Psalm 31

In You, Beloved, I would make my home;
Though I be humiliated with guilt,
    Your mercy and forgiveness will
        deliver me!
Hear me and hasten to my assistance!
For You are my strength and have the power
    to raise me up!

Yes, You are strength and truth to me;
You are my teacher, my guide;
    the Fire of your abiding Love
        cleanses my heart;
Loosen the webs that entangle me,
    that veil my love for You.
Into your Heart I commend my soul.
    You have redeemed me, O Love,
        O ever Faithful One.

Those who put their focus and trust
in false idols
separate themselves from You, O Love.
Though You have seen my guilt
and have noted my wrongdoings,
You have not left me alone with my fears;
rather, You have forgiven my folly
and set my feet on Love's path.
My heartfelt gratitude knows no bounds,
O Gracious Mender of Souls!

Be a comfort to me, Beloved, for I am
in distress;
my eyes are dim from weeping,
my soul is deep with grief.
For my life is worn away with sorrow,
and my years with sighing;
My body has weakened and my bones
waste away with misery.

All my fears rise up to mock me,
my neighbors turn away,
My friends dread to see me and
flee from my sickness of soul.
My mind, too, has left me
like one who is dead;
I have become like a broken vessel.
Yes, I hear the voices around me
whispering of my plight—
fears rise up on every side!
Isolation, rejection, fear surround me
and conspire to overwhelm me.

Still, I trust in You, O Beloved,
I repeat, "You are my Life."

My life is in your hands;
>> deliver me from the fears which
>>> separate me!
Let your face shine on me;
>> hold me in your steadfast love!
Let me know your forgiveness,
>>> O Love,
>> for I call upon You;
>> let my fears be cast out,
>>> let them be transformed.
Let me speak only truth, Beloved,
>> that I might live with integrity,
>>> offering my work and praise to You.

O, how abundant is your goodness,
>> which is ever-present to those
>>> who reverence You,
>> and available to all who make
>>> your Heart their home,
>>> openly for all to see!
Like a mother hen, You shelter them
>>> from temptations of the world;
>> You hold them safe under your wings
>>> from the enemy . . . fear.

Blessed be the eternal Beloved,
>> who wondrously showered me
>>> with steadfast Love
>> when I was overwhelmed by fear.
I had cried out, "Where are You?
>> Have You left me alone forever?"
You heard my fear-filled pleas
>> and enveloped me in Love.

Listen in the silence, all you saints!
>> For Wisdom makes her home there.

The Beloved upholds the faith-filled,
those who embrace goodness
and walk in the Light.
Those who choose to remain in illusion
separate themselves from truth
and know not Love.
Be strong, let your heart take courage
and be encouraged,
all you who would serve
with Love
in the Oneness of Light.

Psalm 32

*B*lessed are you whose wrongdoings
have been forgiven,
whose shame has been forgotten.
Blessed are you in whom Love Divine
finds a home,
and whose spirit radiates truth.

When I acknowledged not my shortcomings,
I became ill through all my defenses.
And day and night, guilt weighed heavy
constricting my heart;
My spirit became dry as desert bones.

I admitted my faults to the Most High,
and I made known my regret;

I cried out, "Forgive me, O Comforter,
for those times I have sinned in
my thoughts, my words,
and my deeds;"
And the Beloved created within me
a clean and open heart.

Therefore, let everyone who is sincere
give thanks to the Beloved;
For whenever we feel paralyzed
by fear,
we shall be embraced by Love.
Dwelling in the Heart of the Beloved,
we are free from distress,
free to live more creatively.

O my Beloved, You are my guide,
You teach me to walk in the Light.
Be watchful of me, counsel me as
I listen to You in the Silence.
I pray for the gifts of inner peace
and wisdom,
For the grace to reverence all of Creation.

Many are the heartaches of those
separated from Love;
Steadfast love abides with those
who surrender their lives into
the hands of the Beloved.
Be glad and rejoice! Let your life
give witness to Love's Way;
And shout for joy, all you upright
of heart!

Psalm 33

Rejoice in the Beloved, O you holy ones!
        Praise is a grace of the loving.
Praise the Beloved with strings and reeds,
Give praise with dance and leaps;
                sing a new song, and
                shout with joyful heart!

For the work of the Creator is truth,
        and all creation reflects the
                faithfulness of the Beloved.
Justice and mercy we render to the Holy One,
To the universe filled with Love Divine.

Through Love Consciousness the heavens
        and earth were created,
And all who dwell on earth
        by the Creator's breath of Life.
All creation, from the distant stars
        to the depth of the seas,
Is held together by the Oneness of Love.

May all the earth reverence the Beloved,
        may everyone stand in awe
                of Love!
For when the Beloved speaks,
        it comes to pass;
As Love's way guides and directs,
        thus, it stands.

Without Love, the nations' counsel
                comes to nothing,
        the plans of the people are futile.

The counsel of the Creator is eternal
available to every generation.
Blessed are the nations that listen
in silence and make decisions
with Wisdom's Counsel;
Blessed are all people who respond
to Love's Way.

For, the Beloved dwells in every heart
that is open and receptive;
Into our hands, into our hearts,
does the Beloved surrender,
that we might do with Love
what we will.
Do we not know, that the nations
are not saved by military might,
just as generals are not saved
by their own strength?
All such arms are the outward expression
of greed in fearful hearts;
They will reap only despair, death,
and destruction.

Behold, the Love of the Beloved is stronger
than ten thousand bombs,
more to be desired than the wealth
of all nations.
Do we not know that to dwell in
the heart of the Beloved
Is the promise to every nation,
the birthright of all people,
the journey to life eternal?

Our soul yearns for the Beloved,
for peace, joy, and assurance.

Then will our hearts be glad and sing
                songs of gratitude,
Praising the name of the Holy One!
May every nation come to live in
            the steadfast Love and Wisdom
                    of the Spirit of Truth!
May all peoples work with Love Divine!

Psalm 34

I will bless the Beloved at all times;
        a song of praise will I sing.
My soul speaks to the Beloved continually;
        let all who suffer hear and be glad.
O, open your hearts, friends,
            that your pain and loneliness
                    be turned to Love;
And then, we shall rejoice in the Beloved
                    together!

When I searched for Love, the Beloved
            answered within my heart,
            and all my fears flew away.
Look to the Beloved, and your
                    emptiness will be filled,
            your face will radiate Love.
For when you weep, the Beloved hears
                    and comes to companion you;
            your burdens are eased by Love.

The Beloved sends angels when you
        call upon these messengers
                for guidance and light,
        for their gracious inspiration,
One with Love, you are never alone!

Happy are all who dwell in the
                Beloved's heart!
Abandon yourself into Love's hands,
                O you holy ones,
For those who give themselves to
                the Beloved,
        lack no good thing.
Everyone separated from Love is empty
                and hungry within;
But those who open their hearts to
                the Beloved,
        are filled to overflowing!

O come and see, come and hear,
        how we honor the Beloved.
Many there are who desire Life,
        who yearn for fulfillment,
        who covet the wisdom of Truth.
Keep your heart open and free,
        take time to dwell in the Silence,
Become a peaceful presence in the world.
For the Beloved sees the deeds
                of our hearts, and
        hears our innermost thoughts.
The face of the Beloved turns from
        the evil ways of men and women;
For Love is kind and merciful and
                remembers not our sins.

Rather, the Beloved is patient,
ever-waiting for us to cry out
for forgiveness.
to embrace Love's way.
How often the Beloved weeps with
compassion
over those who are crushed in spirit.

Though we are beset with many fears
that cause illness and troubles,
The Beloved is ever ready
to comfort us in our sorrows,
to strengthen us on our soul's
journey to wholeness.
The Beloved renews the life of all
who surrender to Love.

Psalm 35

Pray on my behalf, O Beloved, for those
who fight against me;
Forgive on my behalf those who abuse me!
Pour forth your strength into my heart
that I might stand strong!
Encircle with healing love those
who persecute me through fear!
And say to my soul,
"I am with you always!"

Melt the hearts of stone in those
Who seek to kill my body, my spirit.
Turn them around and let them delight
        in your way.
Let their ignorance become as chaff
            before the wind,
        send angels to lead them home to You.
Let their path become filled with light
        that they may see the way of truth!

For without cause they have tried to
            ensnare me;
        without cause they threaten my life.
Surprise them, O Love, with joy!
For ignorance cannot live where your
            love abides;
Let them rise up with a new conscience
        and regret their their past acts
            against others.

Then, O Love, my soul shall rejoice,
        exulting in your goodness.
My whole being shall say,
        "O Beloved, who is like You,
You who give strength to the weak,
            praying on their behalf,
        when fear threatens to overwhelm them,
        holding them back from retaliation
            through your saving love?"

False witnesses rise up, asking me
        questions I cannot answer.
They return my kindness with cruelty;
        my soul weeps.

Yet I, when they were afflicted—
    I lit prayer candles,
    I fasted and sent them help.
I prayed in my simple way as though
    grieving for my family or
      a friend;
I acted as one who grieves a dying mother,
    bowed down and in mourning.

Yet when I stumbled and needed assistance,
    they gathered about me with glee,
    they turned against me;
Even strangers whom I did not know,
    mocked me day and night;
They seemed to gather strength in
      denouncing me,
    and became all the more violent.

How long, O Beloved, must I endure this?
    Rescue me from the oppressors,
    my life from the lions!
I long to give thanks in the great assembly,
    to praise You wherever people gather.

Fill those who rejoice over my plight
      with compassion,
Let peace come to those who hate me
      without cause.
For many desire conflict and war,
    and turn against those who are quiet
      in the land;
    they are driven by greed.
By speaking against me saying, "Aha,
      you are to blame."
    they think to hide their own deceit.

You have seen it all, O Love;
            be silent no longer!
Beloved, stay close beside me!
Hear me, and rise up on my behalf,
       let justice and peace reign!
Yes, O Compassionate One, let truth
            and love overcome ignorance,
            according to your goodness;
      that all might rejoice and give thanks!
Foolish are they to think that persecution
           will bring them joy;
Nor will destruction bring them peace.

Let those who rejoice in another's misfortune,
       in their shame become contrite;
Let them be humbled and turn their hearts
          to You, O Beloved,
        all those who know not Love!
May all who offer their lives to peace
        shout for joy and be glad,
          and always pray,
      "Great are You, O Love, You
      Who dwell in all open hearts!"
Then shall I sing of your saving justice
       and praise You all day long!

Psalm 36

Ignorance lives deep in the hearts
    of those who know not Love;
There is no reverence for Truth
        before their eyes.
For they see themselves as powerful
    and are too proud to see how
    they deceive themselves and others.
They speak not with integrity and
    act not with wisdom and love.
At night their thoughts turn to
        plotting,
    driving them to seek more power;
    fear becomes their constant companion.

Would that they knew that your steadfast
    love, O Holy One,
    extends to the heavens,
    your faithfulness to all the world.
Your saving justice is like the mountains,
    firm and sure,
    your judgments are like the
    mighty deep;
Your Love supports all of creation; yes,
    Your Love Consciousness is everlasting.

How precious is your steadfast love,
    O Companioning Presence.
We, your children, take refuge in
    the shadow of your wings.
We feast on the abundance of Gaia,
    the Earth;
    You invite us to drink from living
    streams of Life.

For in You is the very source of Life;
and in your Light do we see light.

May your steadfast love endure to those
who know You,
your saving grace to those
who love truth and justice!
Protect us from the seeds of arrogance;
the weeds of greed drive away.

Open the hearts of those who live in
darkness, O Beloved,
that they might rise up and live
in the Light of Oneness.

Psalm 37

Give no heed to those who are greedy,
attend not to those who do wrong.
For, like the green grass of spring,
they soon fade and wither away.

Trust in the Most High, and seek goodness;
live harmoniously upon the earth
in peace and with assurance.
Take delight in the Beloved, and
enjoy the bountiful gifts of Love.

Commit your life to the Beloved,
confident that Love will act
on your behalf,

Making clear your pathway,
    bright as the sun at midday.

Be still before the Beloved, and wait
            quietly in the Silence;
        pray for those who prosper by
            deceitful means,
        and for those who live by
            their own devises.

Recognize your own anger as unfulfilled
            desire and,
        lift your thoughts to higher planes;
For those who act out of anger,
        separate themselves from Love;
While those who live in harmony,
        shall know peace, assurance, gratitude,
            and love.

In a little while, those who live with greed,
        will prosper no more;
    the darkness of ignorance will pass,
    as a new dawn enlightens the world.
The lovers of darkness shall perish,
        while the humble shall inherit
            the earth, and find
        delight in sharing its abundance
            with all.

Those who are greedy plot against the weak,
        those without worldly power,
    and rationalize their selfish deeds.
The Beloved watches patiently, knowing
        they will stumble and have to face
            their own downfall.

Those with power make war
           despoiling nations,
        killing the poor and innocent,
              murdering in the name of peace!

O, if they only knew that their greed
           will kill their own spirit;
        their hearts will be broken.

How much better is the little of
           those who know Love, than
        the abundance of the greedy ones.
For the spirit of the selfish will
           be broken;
        while those who live in love,
           shall dwell with Love.

Love walks with the upright,
        and their heritage is forever;
In difficult times, they will be assured,
        even in times of famine,
           their spirits will be filled.
But those who live by usurped power
           will perish;
        Like a refining fire, their deeds
        will burn and vanish away
           in smoke.

Those who are greedy borrow, using
           the assets of others,
        money they cannot pay back;
The upright are generous and give.
Blessed by Love, they know inner peace,
        but the selfish cut themselves
           off from Love.

Our lives come from the Most High
and Love walks beside those with
open hearts;
Those who know Love are blessed and
shall be filled with the Spirit;
though their lives may seem difficult,
Love raises them up.

From my birth to my elder years,
I have watched the upright blessed
with inner strength and faith.
Living as beneficial presences in the world,
their children come to know Love.

Turn from ignorance, and become all that
you were born to be;
thus will you fulfill your birthright.
The Beloved loves justice and will enable
all who call upon Love to grow
in love.
The upright of heart will know the
fulness of life,
their children will be blessed.
Those who give avarice a home,
set their children on the path
that leads to darkness.

The upright of heart know Silence;
when they speak, it is with
wisdom and justice.
For Love abides in their hearts;
their way is made sure.

Those who do wrong look to justify
themselves,
they seek to subdue the upright.

Their greed begets fear and guilt;
    they condemn themselves.
Closing their hearts to Love,
    they live unaware of their own
        deep poverty of heart.

Desire only Love and walk your days
        with the Beloved;
    you will radiate with joy, blessing
      others with Love's presence;
    you will know not loneliness with
      Love's Companioning Presence.

I have seen the greedy ones, their
      ways are overbearing,
    they puff themselves up with pride.
When I pass them, I see only
      an inflated balloon;
    even so, I take time to honor
      the Divine Spark hidden
        within them.

Look at the innocent, consider those
      honest of heart;
    they leave a rich inheritance
    to their children.
But those who live with greed, end
      their days empty,
    they leave a legacy of hollow vanity
    to their children.

The saving grace of the upright comes
      from the Beloved;
    Love is their refuge in times of
    trouble.

Love leads the way and they arrive
    home safely,
        delivered from those who tempt them
            with power.
Love invites all to open their hearts.

Psalm 38

O Beloved, in your mercy, forgive me,
        in your compassion raise me up!
For arrows of fear pierce my heart,
        and guilt weighs heavy upon me.

I live in confusion, fear, and despair
        because of my illusions;
My body responds with illness
        because of my stubbornness.
Ignorance casts me into darkness;
        I grope in every direction,
            searching in vain.

Because of foolishness, my heart has
            turned to stone,
I am utterly bowed down, overcome
            with remorse;
        I spend my days in mourning,
        and pray for mercy throughout
            the night.
I acknowledge my weakness,
            O Loving Presence,
        illness has overtaken me.

My energy is depleted, my spirit
        crushed;
    I groan under the tumult of
        my heart.

Beloved, all my longing is known to You,
    my sighing is not hidden
        from You.
My heart throbs endlessly, my
        strength fails me;
    even the light of my eyes—
        it also has disappeared.
My friends and companions have
        no time for me,
    my family stays at a distance.

The tempter knows well my weakness
    and lays a snare in my path,
Those who choose the darkness are
        ever at my door,
        seeking my company.

Like someone who is deaf,
        I do not hear,
    like one who is dumb,
        I do not speak.
Yes, I pretend not to hear, because
    I am afraid to rebuke those
        who lead me astray.

For You alone, Beloved, do I wait;
    You alone, O Gracious One,
        will answer my cry.
I pray, "Be my strength!
    Uphold me when I am weak
        and paralyzed with fear!"

For I seem ready to fall,
>   my pain is always with me.
I confess my shortcomings,
>   I am sorry for my transgression.
No longer will I listen and follow
>   the ego's wily ways;
>   they lead only to despair and
>   separate me from Love.
I feel like a child again, ready
>   to learn life's lessons of peace;
>   I choose to walk in the Light.

I no longer feel separated from You,
>   O Beloved!
>   I know I am One with All!
You have rolled away the stone
>   from my heart,
>   O Love, my Beloved Friend!

Psalm 39

I prayed, "Be Thou my voice,
>   that I may not err with
>   my tongue;
I will remain mute, so long
>   as my fears assail me."
I was silent in my ignorance,
>   I held my peace to no avail;

My distress grew worse,
my heart burned within me.
As I mused, the fire burned;
finally, I spoke with my tongue.

"O Loving Presence, You are with us
to the end,
whatever the measure of our days;
our life passes by as the
blinking of an eye!
For the gift of life fades too
soon away,
yet how precious are we
in your sight!
Surely your Plan for us is
written on our hearts!
Surely your angels stand ready
to guide us on our way!
Surely there is nothing to fear, for
You abide within us; You
await patiently for us to
awaken to your Love."

And now, O Loving Friend, for what
do I wait?
My hope is in your guidance.
Forgive me for all my mistakes;
let me not walk in ignorance!
I stand silent before You, I hold
my tongue;
to You I turn in repentance.
Remove the blemishes from my heart;
for I am weary of guilt.
When you blot out the darkness
of sin,
burning it with refining fire,

Surely, I am made new, redeemed by
your Love!

Hear my prayer, O Listening Heart,
give ear to my cry;
wash away my tears
with your peace!
For I am but a passing guest,
a sojourner on this earth
as in all generations.
Look upon me with mercy, that I
may know the joy
of living in the realm of Love,
now and in the Life to come.
Amen.

Psalm 40

I waited patiently for the Beloved,
who heard my cry and
came to me.
Love raised me from the pits of
despair,
out of confusion and fear,
and set my feet upon a rock.
making my steps secure.
There is a new song in my mouth,
a song of praise to the Beloved.

May many see and rejoice, may they
          put their trust in Love.

Blessed are those who make Love
               their home,
          who do not turn to the proud,
          to those who follow false idols!
O Beloved, how wondrous are your gifts
               to us; your thoughts are
               beyond our imagination.
          What joy to live in Oneness with You!
Were we to proclaim and tell of Your
               beauty and blessed grace,
          who could measure it?

Sacrifice and offering are not
               your desire for us;
          for, you have opened our
               heart's ear.
Burnt offerings are not required.
My heart affirms my surrender;
          in the Book of Life it is written:
"I abandon myself into your hands,
          for I love You and wish only
               to create with You,
                    O my Beloved;
For You are the Life of my life forever."

I tell the glad news of
               Love's way
          to all who will listen.
Yes, I raise my voice,
          with praise and acclamation.
I tell of Love's saving grace
               within my heart,
          I speak of Love's faithfulness
               and healing power.

I aspire to reveal your steadfast love
        and truth
      through the witness of my life.
Do not, O Beloved, withhold
      your mercy from me,
Let your Love, your Light,
            and faithfulness ever
      guide and uphold me.
For fears so often overwhelm me;
My desires and anger cause me
        to be blind; so
I look away when I see injustice,
      my heart becomes cold.

In your mercy, O Beloved, deliver me!
        O Love, make haste to help me!
Let my fears be put to rest,
        fears that separate me from You;
Let all that keeps me from love,
            from peace and gratitude,
      be transformed within me.

And may all who seek Love
      rejoice and be glad;
May all who would live truth
        and justice,
      continually call upon Love!
As for me, though often broken
        and weak,
      I know that Love dwells within.
For now, where injustice or illusion
            make their home,
      I witness to your Peace and Love,
        O Teacher and Friend to All!

Psalm 41

Who among us hears the cry of the poor?
How many open their hearts
and heed the Call?
The plight of the world is a wound
to the very Heart of Love,
a scar on our own souls.
Blessed are those who lovingly respond!
The Friend, who knows all hearts,
will remember their kindness.
They will know joy, peace, and deep
fulfillment working in harmony
with all who serve toward healing
the needs of this troubled world.

As for me, I prayed, "O Soul Mender,
be gracious unto me.
For I have been deaf to those in need;
my fears paralyzed me.
I am bound like a prisoner held
in my own house,
alone and abandoned.
Each fear I push away or deny
rises up with power;
feeling anxious, lies and deceipt
take the place of truth.
I can hide no longer; my confusion,
the way I blame others,
have turned even my friends away."

"O Divine Healer, help me face the fears
that threaten to overwhelm me;
without your guidance, they will
bring about what I most fear!

I am on my knees asking forgiveness;
   give me strength to turn all
      that separates me from You
      into love and kindness.
You, who are Unconditional Love, You
   do not judge our weaknesses;
      raise me up, that I may be renewed
         in body, mind, and soul!"

By this I know that You have
      graciously forgiven me;
   fear did not triumph over me,
      though my heart was broken open
         so the light could enter in.
You upheld me, filled me with integrity,
      and opened my heart to the poor.

Blessed be the Beloved, loving Presence
      to all hearts open to Love,
      from everlasting to everlasting!
         Amen.

Psalm 42

As a hart longs for flowing streams,
   so longs my soul for You,
      O Beloved.
My soul thirsts for the Beloved,
   for the Living Water.

When may I come and behold
            your face?
Tears have been my only nourishment
            day and night,
While friends ask continually,
        "Why do you seem so lost
                and forlorn?"

All this I remembered,
        as I poured out my soul:
How I knew your Presence within me
        as I went out among the throng,
        proceeding to the House of Prayer;
With loud voice we gave You praise
                and acclamation,
            a multitude proclaiming gratitude
                and joy.
Why are you cast down, O my soul,
        and why are you disquieted
                within me?
My hope is in the Beloved, my
            strength and my joy,
            O my soul, open the door to Love!

My soul is cast down within me,
        yet I remember You
From my mother's womb to maturity,
        through all the days of my life.
Deep calls to deep
        at the thunder of your waterfalls;
All your waves and your billows
        have washed over me.
By day You lead me in steadfast
                love;
        at night your song is within me,
        prayer from the Heart of my heart.

I say to the Beloved, the Blessed One,
    "Why have You forgotten me?
Why go I mourning because of
            the oppression of fear?"
As with a deadly wound in
            my body,
I feel the pain of war and injustice;
    while the powerful seem to destroy,
    the innocent seem of no account.

O my soul, let not the quagmire of war
    keep me from radiating your peace,
    your love and light to the world.
My hope is in You, O Spirit of Truth;
    be my strength and my guide.
O my soul, let us celebrate the Oneness
            of all Creation!

Psalm 43

Bring justice to the people,
            O Beloved,
    and strength on my behalf
    to stand firm against oppression;
From all that is greedy and unjust
            deliver me!
For You are the One in whom I
        take refuge; yet,
    Have You abandoned me?

Why go I mourning because of the
　　　　　　oppression of ignorance?

O, send out your light and your truth;
　　　　　let them guide me,
Let them lead me to your holy altar,
　　　to the inner home of integrity!
Then will I know You, Heart of my heart,
　　　my exceeding joy;
And I will praise You with song,
　　　O my Beloved, my Awakener.

Why are you cast down, O my soul,
　　　　and why are you disquieted within me?
My hope is in the Beloved, my strength
　　　　　　and my joy,
　　　O my soul, open the door to Love!
Yes! Let us sing a song of diversity,
　　　a song of Oneness and Unity!
For we are all One in Love's Heart,
　　　　　　now and forevermore.
Let us ever reflect the Peace we are!

Psalm 44

We have heard with our ears,
　　　　O Rock of ages,
　　　all generations have proclaimed

The mighty deeds You wrought
          in their days,
       in the days of old;
Of how You with your own hand
          drove out the nations,
       sowing seeds for new life;
Of how You led the peoples
          into bondage,
       and then You set them free;
For not by their own might did
          they win the land,
       nor did their own strength give
          them victory,
But by your power and your might,
       and the light of your countenance;
       for You sought to awaken them!

O, You who know all hearts,
       who are ever-present to your people,
Through You we face our enemies;
       through your Name we call forth
          our fears.
For not in military powers do we trust,
       nor can arms save us.
For only in You can we put
          our fears to rest,
       and transform them into peace.
In you, O Gracious One, do we give thanks,
       and forever will we offer You
          our songs of praise.

Yet at times You seem to abandon us,
       leaving us alone with our fears.
You have given us the freedom
          to turn from You;
       then does our ego seek to rule the day.

We become as sheep for slaughter,
    straying far from the fold.
You seem to require too little of us,
    remaining mute as we wander
        on worldly highways.

Without your saving grace, we come in
        conflict with our neighbors,
    we fear all who seem different
        from us.
We seek to better ourselves at the expense
    of other nations,
    we become arrogant and greedy.
Our spirit weakens as we attack others,
        we become deaf and blind
To the cries of those oppressed,
    at the sight of those wronged.

As all this comes upon us, we finally
        remember You, O Infinite Love,
    we pray for your strength in all
        of our hopes and challenges.
Our hearts recall your promises of old:
        to be with us always. Yet,
Deep darkness overshadows the land.

Until crises come, we forget the Name
    of the Creator;
    we spread forth our hands to
    a worldly god.
Yet, can we ever hide from You, O Beloved?
    For You know the secrets, the will,
        of our hearts and mind.
No, Love does not abandon us;
    we ourselves turn our faces
        from the Light.

Rouse yourself! Why do you sleep,
      O foolish peoples?
     Awaken! Do not stray in the darkness
       forever!
Why do you cover your faces?
     Why are you ashamed and cast down?
With your souls bowed down to the
       dust,
     call out to the Beloved for forgiveness.
Rise up, pray for a change of heart!
     Then will the Indwelling Presence,
      the Divine Guest,
     awaken you with kindly Love!

Psalm 45

I address my verses to the
      Heart of all hearts;
My tongue is like the pen
      of a ready scribe.
My heart overflows with gratitude
      and peace;

You are the lodestar for humankind;
     grace springs forth from your Love;
     You, who are closer than our breath,
      speak to us from the silence.
     Those who listen and heed are
       blessed beyond belief!

Put on the voice of authority,
        O Beloved, speak to us in
        your glory and grandeur!

With mercy and strength go forth
      for the cause of Truth to
        teach Love's way;
      with resolute authority awaken
        your people toward wholeness!
Your ways are narrow, and few there are
        who choose to follow;
      many stumble and fall all
        along the Way.

Your Divine Presence endures forever
        and ever.
      Your sovereign edict is ordained
        with justice;
      your love is unconditional,
        without reserve.
Therefore, O Creator, O Heart of Love,
        anoint us with
      the oil of gladness to share
        with all;
      your raiment is as fragrant blossoms,
        fruit of the earth,
      healing herbs from nature's bounty.
From every direction stringed instruments
        will gladden our hearts;
      our friends will be mature and kind,
        filled with integrity,
      standing beside us in times of need.

Hear, O peoples, consider, and
        incline your ear;

forget what has gone before you;
turn your feet to the path of Love.
Open your hearts to the Beloved,
learn of humility, be blessed
even in brokenness,
For those are the treasures stored
in eternity.

All glorious is the soul within,
the abode of the Merciful One;
through many trials and suffering
do you come to the Beloved,
refined by fire as you follow
Love's way.
With joy and gladness you are led along,
as you awaken to the Heart
of your heart.

Instead of a house of fear, you
will come to dwell with Love,
you will radiate the light of truth
to all the earth.
There will you celebrate the Beloved
for all generations to come,
the people will praise Love's way
for ever and ever.

Psalm 46

The Beloved is our refuge and our strength,
    a Loving Presence in times of trouble.
Therefore we need not fear though
        the earth should change,
    though the mountains shake in the
        heart of the sea;
Though its waters roar and foam,
    though the mountains tremble
        with its tumult.

There is a river whose streams
        make glad the Holy City,
    the holy habitation of the Most High.
The Beloved is in the midst of it,
        it shall not be moved;
    Our loving Creator is an
        ever-present help.
The nations may be at war,
        countries left in ruins,
    yet is the Voice of the Almighty
        heard, slowly breaking through
        hearts of stone.
The Beloved is ever with us,
    the infinite Heart of Love.

Come, behold the works of the Beloved,
    how love does reign even in
        humanity's desolation.
For the Beloved yearns for wars to cease,
    shining light into fearful hearts; loving
    even those who oppress the weak,
        refining hearts of steel!

"Be still and know that I am Love.
　　Awaken! Befriend justice and mercy;
　　Do you not know you bear my Love?
　　　　Who among you will respond?"
O Blessed One, You know all hearts,
　　You are ever with us;
　　may Love ever guide our lives!

Psalm 47

Clap you hands, people of all nations!
Acclaim the Creator with joyful songs!
　　Rejoice in the beauty of diversity!
The Beloved of our hearts is mighty,
　　reigning over all of Creation:
　　　　the lands, sea, and air.
Love Consciousness invites all people
　　　　to co-creation,
　　the nations to peace.
Love Consciousness is our hearitage,
　　　our birthright,
　　to be awakened in every soul.

Let the Love you are sing praises
　　　with loud acclamation;
　　join the cosmic dance of celebration!
Sing praises to the Creator,
　　Sing praises to the Beloved,
　　　sing praises, one and all!

For Love Consciousness created the universe,
let us dance to the flute
and the harp.
Love Consciousness hovers over the nations,
awaiting our awakening to Love.
May the leaders of all nations
gather as One,
choosing to walk in peace.
For Earth is made of Love and Light;
abandoning ourselves to your Will,
we can choose the path of healing.
We sing songs of gratitude for Earth:
our home, to You,
O Great Healer, Life of our lives.

Psalm 48

Great is the Beloved and greatly
to be praised
in the abode of the Most High!
The holy mountain, beautiful
in elevation,
is the joy of all the earth;
Clear as a crystal within its
pearly gates,
Within the stronghold of open hearts,
the Beloved's voice can be heard.
For lo, the inner fears assembled,
they came forth together.

As soon as they saw the Beloved,
>they were in panic, they took
>>to flight;
Trembling before the eyes of Love,
>they labored for a stronghold.
Through the Heart's ear, the Word
>can be heard,
The refining Fire of Divine Mercy
>melted hearts held in bondage
>>by fear and illusion,
In the abode of the Most High,
>where the Beloved lives forever.

We have pondered your steadfast
>love, O Beloved,
>in the midst of our hearts,
>your Holy Temple.
We call on your Name, O Holy One,
>and praise You to the ends
>>of the earth.
Your Word is our armor of strength
>let us rejoice and be glad!
Let all peoples rejoice because
>of your forgiving love!
See with your heart's eye
>the crystal mountain,
>note the clarity and purity within;
Consider well the essence of love,
>the echoes of mercy and justice,
That you may tell the generations
>to come
>that this is the Beloved,
>our hope for ever and ever.
Yes, the Blessed One will be with us
>for ever!

Psalm 49

*H*ear this, all nations!
Give ear, all inhabitants of the
        earth,
    both low and high,
    rich and poor together!
My mouth shall speak wisdom!
    the meditation of my heart
        shall be understanding.
I will incline my ear to the Word;
    I will solve my problems
        through the whispers
        of the Heart's voice.

Why should I give up in times
        of trouble,
    when stubborn fears oppress me,
        when illusion surrounds me,
Fears that can give birth to greed
    and lead to exploitation?

Truly I cannot save myself,
    or offer a haven of peace to
        another,
When my home is like a hornet's nest,
    a hive of restless fears.
Turning to you, O Guiding Spirit,
    is my strength and support,
    a stronghold in times of trouble.

Yes, even the wise are not immune
        to fear;
    yet, unlike the ignorant, the wise
        face their fears with resolve.

Not running away, nor projecting them
onto others,
They trace them to the source,
rooting them out as weeds
from a rose garden.
Thus, they do not trust in the riches
of the world,
but in the Treasure hidden
within the heart.

Others are arrogant in their ignorance,
proud of their own counsel.
Like sheep led to slaughter,
their fears compel them to
walk in the darkness,
Guiding them onto unholy paths,
into webs of intrigue,
where despair and destruction
make their home.
Yet does the Spirit of Truth abide within,
veiled by bulwarks of pain.

Be not afraid to discover the Treasure
within,
to seek the gold hidden in
the garden of your heart.
For inasmuch as you root out
each fear,
will truth and peace and joy
become your riches.
You will live in the realm of Love
becoming a light,
a beneficial presence in the world.
Future generations will be blessed,
the bonds of ignorance
broken forever.

O Spirit of Truth, You are our strength
and our guiding light,
Lead us, O Love, to the eternal Treasure,
the Heart of all hearts.

Psalm 50

The Beloved, through the energy of Love,
brought forth the world.
From the rising to the setting sun,
Love radiates out to all the nations
perfect in beauty.
The Beloved has come and will not
keep silence; for
Divine Love is a consuming Fire,
calling forth heaven and earth
to the judgment of all peoples:
"Gather around, my loyal friends,
all who by repentance and recompense
follow the Inner Way."
The universe forever proclaims justice,
And, the Beloved's Indwelling Presence
guides those who hear with
their heart's ear.

"Listen, all people, and I shall speak;
I will bear witness against you,
O nations:
As Divine Presence, Eternal Flame of Love,

Shall I not find fault with what
          you call holy,
          these offerings of greed and war
          that are before Me always?
Your lies and deceitful ways,
          your greed for power and wealth
          are spawned by darkness.
Have you forgotten that we are to be
          One in Love and Truth,
          that all of life is Sacred Gift?
I know every creature, every plant,
          every mineral;
I know you—your every need
          and your fears;
The Earth and all that is in it
          belongs to the Whole, to be
          tended by all in co-operation
          with Love.
Shall I accept your proud and
          boasting hearts,
          the oppression, the injustices
          brought about
          through your fearful deeds?
Never shall I accept such burnt offerings!
Rather, offer to the Beloved a gift
          of thanksgiving
          with grateful hearts;
For what other return can you make
          for all that Love offers to you?
My friends, srearch for the still voice
          that dwells in the Silence.
If you call upon Me in times of trouble,
I am ever present to you.
          You will know Me in your hearts,
          as you honor my love for you.
To you, whose hearts have turned
          to stone I say:

"What right have you to mouth empty prayers,
and make so free with words
attributed to Love—
You, who hate correction and turn away
when you hear my Voice speaking
within your heart?
You rob the poor with your greed
and prejudice;
You consort with murder and destruction;
You blame others for your own
deceitful ways,
thinking I am blind to your
iniquities.
The air, the earth, and the seas
have become foul with the pollution
of your self-seeking ways
in the name of nationalism, security,
and progress.
All this you have done, and shall
I keep silence?
You think that I am another like yourself,
but, point by point, I shall
rebuke you to your face.
Think well on this, you who disdain
Divine Love;
for you will reap in proportion
the suffering that you have sown,
and no one will be able to save you
from your own destruction."

All who surrender to the love of
the Great Mystery,
whose hearts are merciful and kind,
will go in beauty and walk with grace;
And all who reverence Love's Eternal Flame,
will know Love's Companioning Presence.

Psalm 51

Have mercy on me, O Gracious One,
    according to your steadfast love;
According to your abundant kindness
      forgive me where my thoughts and
          deeds have hurt others.
Lead me in the paths of justice,
    guide my steps on paths of peace!

Teach me, that I may know my weaknesses,
    the shortcomings that bind me,
The unloving ways that separate me,
      that keep me from recognizing
        your Life in me;
For, I keep company with fear, and
    dwell in the house of ignorance.
Yet, I was brought forth in love,
    and love is my birthright.

You have placed your truth in the
        inner being;
    therefore, teach me the wisdom
      of the heart.
Forgive all that binds me in fear,
      that I might radiate love;
    cleanse me that your light might
      shine in me.
Fill me with gladness; help me to
    transform weakness into strength.
Look not on my past mistakes
    but on the aspirations
      of my heart.

Create in me a clean heart, O Gracious One,
    and put a new and right spirit
      within me.

Enfold me in the arms of Love, and
    fill me with your Holy Spirit.
Restore in me the joy of your saving grace,
    and encourage me with a new spirit.

Then I will teach others your ways,
    and prisoners of fear will return
      to You.
Deliver me from the addictions of society,
    O Healer of souls,
    keep me from temptation that
    I may tell of your justice
      and mercy.

O Gracious One, open my lips and
    my mouth shall sing forth
      your praise.
For You do not want sacrifice;
    You delight in our friendship
      with You.
A sacrifice most appropriate is a
      humble spirit;
    a repentant and contrite heart;
      O Merciful One,
    receive our gratitude and love.

Let the nations turn from war,
    and encourage one another as
      good neighbors.
O Blessed and Compassionate Friend,
    melt our hearts of stone,
    break through the fears that
      lead us into darkness, and
Guide our steps toward the way of peace.

Psalm 52

Why do you boast, O proud peoples,
    of your decisions that hurt the poor?
    All day long, you plan exploitation.
Lies are on your tongue as
    you turn from the truth.
You love riches more than justice,
    burying your heads in sand
        like the ostrich,
So you are deaf to the cries of
        the oppressed, blind
        to their impoverishment.

Yet justice will prevail in the end;
    your riches will turn to rags,
    you will die separated from Love.
Those who live in truth, will know
    the joy of Love Divine.
They will see the emptiness of those
    who turn from Love,
    who put their trust in
        abundant riches,
    who seek security in wealth.

Blessed are those who are like
        the strong oak
  in the house of the Beloved.
Blessed are those who trust in
    the gentle love of the Counselor
        and hear the Voice of Love.
Gratitude flows from their hearts
    as they walk in truth, as
    they live in unity and peace
    in the presence of the Beloved.

Psalm 53

Those lacking in understanding may say,
  "There is no Divine Presence."
They have not yet opened their hearts
        to the Divine Guest,
    to the Beloved, who dwells within.

The Holy Spirit seeks our hearts
        that have been broken,
Ever ready to heal them with
        strength and new life.

Even when a heart remains closed,
        seeking its own will,
The Beloved waits with abiding courtesy
        to hear the inward call.

Many there are who know not Love,
        laboring only for money and power,
Becoming greedy and dissatisfied,
        oppressing the poor and
            the weak.

There they are; fear besets them—
        fear that others will steal their
            wealth,
        that their riches will be scattered
            and lost;
        they live in prisons of their own
            making.

O, that deliverance would come to them!
        For, when they seek the Treasure
            within,
        they will be blessed and know
                the joy, friendship, and love
                of the Beloved in all hearts.

Psalm 54

Awaken me, O Blessed Healer with
    your holy mercy,
      that I might be free of fear.
Hear my prayer, O Holy One;
    give ear to the words of
        my mouth.

For nagging doubts assail me,
    bringing loneliness and pain;
I remember not the Beloved, so
    overwhelming are my fears.

Yet behold, You are my helper,
    the upholder of my life.
With You I have the strength to
      face my fears;
    Your faithfulness will help me
      transform them into love.

With boundless confidence, I
    abandon myself into your Heart;
    I give praise to your holy Name,
      O Beloved,
    with gratitude and joy.
For You deliver me from my illusions,
    and, through Love, my heart
      opens to Wisdom.

Psalm 55

Give ear to my prayer, O Beloved,
    and hide not from my
        supplication!
Listen to me, and answer me; for,
    I am overwhelmed by anxiety,
I am tormented by the wily voice
    of my doubts;
        the oppression of my illusions
        confuse me.
They keep me bound in a prison,
        and, like bad company,
    they enclose me in darkness.

My heart is in anguish within me,
    thoughts of death keep me
        company.
I spend my hours in fear and
        trembling,
    and despair never leaves me.
I cry out, "O that I had wings
    like a dove!
    I would fly away and be at rest;
Yes, I would flee far from my fears,
    I would lodge in the country,
I would hasten to find shelter from
    the raging doubts and anger."

Stand with me, O Beloved, clear all
    the confusion that dwells within;
    for darkness and conflict dwell
    within my soul.
Day and night fears attack without
    warning;

My heart is weak in the midst of
        this suffering,
    the end seems near at hand.
Oppression and ignorance do not depart
    where truth is a stranger.

It is not a specific doubt that
        taunts me—
    then I could bear it;
It is not a known fear that rises up
        within—
    then I could face it.
No, in my deepest being, I feel that
        You have abandoned me.
We use to hold sweet converse together;
    within the Silence we walked in
        harmony and peace.
Let my prayer be heard, O Comforter.
    Listen to me, and answer me; for,
    I cry out to You in the midst
        of my pain!

Yes, I call upon the Beloved, knowing
    that Love will heed my cry.
From morning through the evening
    I moan in my loneliness,
    and surrender myself to Love.
The Beloved will deliver my soul
        in safety
    and give me strength to search
        within,
    to find the source of my fear.
Love's presence will make itself
        known to me,
    bringing comfort and stilling
        this disquiet within.

With gentle and tender guidance
    I shall find my way Home.

Fear and doubt sought to capture me,
    weaving webs of confusion,
    breeding lairs of anxiety.
Sowing false seeds of empty promises,
    they sought to take control.
Yet You, O Beloved, were ever near,
    waiting for me to call upon You.

I offered my fears up to the Beloved,
    and Love heard my cry;
I sought the One who ever listens;
    once again, I knew Love's Presence.

Yes, You, O Beloved, bring my fears
    to the fore,
    exposing them to the Light;
I abandon myself into your hands,
Into your Heart I commend my soul,
    in You will I place my heart.

Psalm 56

Be gracious to me, O Merciful Love,
    for I dread the power of others;
    all day long my fears consume me;

I am like a door mat that people
        step upon;
    to oppose another's will seems
        too much for me.
Now, when I am afraid, I put
        my trust in You.
In You, O Guide and Comforter,
    I find the strength to act.
    What can others do to me?

Too often I succumb to invitations
        not in my best interest;
        I do that which I know can only
        lead to harm.
Others know of my weakness; they
        watch my downfall.
Only with You by my side,
        O Rock,
        will I find courage to choose
        new life.
        In your saving grace, answer
        my prayer, O Beloved!

If You had kept count of my
        transgressions,
        Your tears could fill a lake!
        Are they not in your book?
Now my fears will be turned back,
        in the day when I call.
This I know, that the Beloved
        dwells within.
In You, whose Love I praise,
        in the Holy One, whose Light
        I praise,

In You I shall trust without fear.
What can others do to me?

My vows to You I must uphold,
O Beloved;
I give You thanks; my heart
overflows with gratitude.
For You deliver me from the depths
of despair.
Yes, my fears You help me
to face;
they are put to rest,
That I may walk with You,
O Beloved,
into the light of a new dawn.

Psalm 57

Be merciful to me, O Beloved!
I open my heart to You,
for in You is Love and Wisdom.
In the shadow of your wings I will
find peace,
until the fears that bind me
are transformed.
I cry to the Source of all life,
to the Eternal One whose Plan
is wholeness for all.

Send your angels to awaken me,
put to rest all that keeps me
in darkness.
Help me to live the Oneness we are
eternally with Love Consciousness!

I lie at night in the midst of
dragons,
fears that seek to overpower me;
They rise up to taunt me,
they seek to control my life.

Be exalted, O Holy One, Creator of
the galaxies!
Let your Glory, your Love and Light
embrace all the earth!

My fears have woven a web; like a
spider that seeks
to entrap and eat me.
Fears live within me, gnawing at
my bones,
they bring only suffering, despair,
and paralysis.

Yet in my heart I know, Beloved, your
Love is the healing balm for fear.
I will sing and make melody!
Awaken, my soul!
Awaken me to Love's song!
I yearn to co-create with you.
I give thanks to You among
the peoples,
O Heart of my heart;

I sing praises to You among
          the nations.
For your enduring Love and Light
      fills the universe, and even
      makes a home in my heart!

Be exalted, O Holy One, Creator of
          the galaxies!
      For your Glory reigns throughout
      all the universe!

Psalm 58

Do the leaders of the nations know
          what is right? Or
      are their hearts set on power
          and fame?
Do they look within for guidance, to
          the Heart of all hearts?
      In whom can the people
          put their trust?

The ignorant go astray, following
          idol gods of illusion;
      they err in their blindness,
          fooling only themselves.
They are filled with conceit and
      empty promises.

As the hunter with sweet bait
       lures the deer with intent
              to kill,
The weak become food for the arrogant.

O Beloved, open our eyes;
       break through the darkness of
              our ignorance,
              tear down the walls of our fear!
Let us trust in the Divine Moment,
       living as children with trust
              and joy.
Let us awaken to our birthright,
       free to choose the creative path,
       walking in harmony to the
              planetary song.
Awaken us to the interconnectedness
              of all beings,
       to all that fly and swim,
       to all that walk and crawl
              upon the earth!

Those who know Love will rejoice as
       the nations learn to cooperate,
       as the peoples of earth recover
              their true heritage.
People will say, "The time has come
       to dwell in peace and integrity;
       to walk together in the Light
              of the Most High,
              Heart of the Universe!"

Psalm 59

Awaken me from my fears,
      O my Beloved,
        give me strength to face them
        as they rise up within me;
Let your Love envelop me,
      and direct my thoughts to
          peaceful paths.
Where I have erred in thought and
         spoken in anger,
      where I have acted without love,
        I ask forgiveness.

Rouse yourself, come to my aid,
        heed my cry!
      For You are the Compassionate One,
        Comforter to all who ask.
You come to those who seek You;
      O Mender of broken hearts,
         create a new heart within me.
I long to sleep at night in peace,
      to awaken to a new dawn.
Too long have my fears, my guilt,
        pursued me,
      whispering lies in my ears
      and evoking beguiling images
        of illusionary darkness.

Yes, In You, O my Beloved, I find
      rest; I am strong.
      You remember not my erring ways,
      Your forgiveness is forever.
O my Strength, I will sing praises
      to You;
      for You are my Rock.

With steadfast Love, You stand
with me;
You teach me to face my fears;
they disappear in the Light.
Cast them not out, but help me
face them;
give me courage to let them go
one by one,
O Comforter, my Strength!
Let me make amends and start anew;
help me grow in wisdom and
understanding.
For the havoc that my fears wield
within me,
turns to chaos in my life,
wounding others and leading to
a living death.

Then, as I become free of fear
I will live in harmony,
Love will shine through, and
people will know that You live
in my heart.
At night I will rest in the Heart
of the Beloved,
my days will be guided
by Love.
My thoughts will become prayers
offered from the Silence
deep within.

O, how I will sing of your kindness;
I will sing aloud of your
Love for All!

For You have been my rock
        and my refuge in the days
            of my distress.
O Blessed Heart, I sing my songs
            of love to You,
        for You, O Beloved, have
            renewed my life;
You have set me free to live
            with gratitude and joy!

Psalm 60

O Beloved, why do I believe that
        I can separate myself
            from You, feeling like
        an alien in a foreign land?
        O, that I might return to
            the Light.
You know how I tremble with fear;
        help me to break down the walls,
        to let go of illusions, for
            I want to stand tall.
You have allowed me to suffer
            hard things;
        You have not prevented my
            downfall.
You, who are Love, gave me leeway
            to choose,
        to wander far from home.

O my Beloved, be gracious unto me,
   welcome me back into new life,
      hear my prayer!

The Comforter came to me:
   "With joy are you ever at home
      in my Heart,
   as I have always lived in yours.
You are mine; I belong to you;
   the broken are blessed with
      humility,
   the wayward who turn back
      walk with me as love,
      walk with me knowing Love.
Let your mind be guided by truth,
   your heart informed by wisdom;
      then will you know peace and joy."

Who will enter the Heart of Love?
   Who will open their hearts and
      know the Beloved?
Who dares to face their fears, to
   break down the prison walls,
      to walk with Love?
O grant us help to answer the call,
   strengthen us with pure resolve!
With the Beloved we shall triumph;
   with Love we shall be free!

Psalm 61

*H*ear my cry, O Merciful One,
    listen to my prayer;
From the depths of my being
      I call to You,
    for my heart is faint.

Lead me to the Rock that is
      my strength,
    for You alone are my refuge,
    your steadfast Love conquers
      my fears.
Let me dwell in your Heart forever!
    O, to be safe under the shelter
      of your wings!
For with tender Love, You have
      heard my prayers,
    You have shown me the heritage
      of those who know your Love
      and Friendship.

Committed to my birthright, I will
      serve You in this world and
      in the Unseen Realm of Love.
    As I walk on your path forever,
      You fill me with abiding love,
      gentle joy, deep peace,
      and wisdom.

I shall sing praises and blessings
      to your Name, as
    I abandon myself into your Heart
    moment by moment.
    For You are the Love and Mind
    of our galaxy!

Psalm 62

For You alone my soul waits in silence;
    from the Beloved comes my salvation.
Enfolding me with strength and steadfast love,
    my faith shall remain firm.

Yet, how long will fear rule my life,
    holding me in its grip like
      a trembling child,
      a dark and lonely grave?
Fear keeps me from living fully, from
      sharing my gifts;
    it takes pleasure in imprisoning
      my soul.
Fear pretends to comfort, so long
      has it dwelled within me;
    truly, it is my enemy.

For You alone my soul waits in silence;
    my hope is from the Beloved.
Enfolding me with strength and
      steadfast love,
    my faith shall remain firm.
In the Silence rests my freedom and
      my guidance; for
You are the Heart of my heart,
    You speak to me in the Silence.

Trust in Love at all times, O people
    pour out your heart to the Beloved;
    Let Silence be a refuge for you.
Being of low estate is but a sigh,
    being of high estate is misleading;

In the balance, either high or low,
     it is of little consequence—
          they are gone in one breath.
Riches, whether obtained by right
          or through extortion,
          rarely lead to nought but greed—
     set not your heart on them.

Once You have spoken,
     twice have I heard:
Our potential gifts belong to You;
     to You, O Beloved, belongs our
          faithful love.
For You render to us all that
     we offer to You—
          fear begets fear,
          love begets love.
For You alone my soul waits in silence;
     from the Beloved comes Life,
          Love and Light.

Psalm 63

O Love, You are my Beloved, and
          I long for You,
     my soul thirsts for You;
All that is within me thirsts,
     as in a dry and barren land
          with no water.

So I have called out to You in
          my heart,
     sensing your power and glory.
Because your wondrous Love is
          Life in me,
     my lips will praise You.
I would radiate your Love as long
          as I live,
     becoming a blessing to others
          in gratitude to You.

My soul feasts as with a
          magnificent banquet,
     and my mouth praises You with
          joyful lips,
When I ponder on your kindness, and
     meditate on You throughout
          the night;
For You have been my salvation,
     and in the shadows of your wings
          I sing for joy.
My soul clings to You,
     your love upholds me.
The fears that seem to separate me
          from You
     shall be transformed and
          disappear;
As they are faced, each fear
          is diminished;
     they shall be gone as in a dream
          when I Awaken.
And my soul shall rejoice in the
          Beloved.
     All who open their hearts to Love
          will live in peace and joy!

Psalm 64

O You who hear all hearts, hear
    my plea;
    preserve my life when fears
      beset me,
    when the pangs of jealousy pierce
      like a two-edged sword,
When doubts rise up and leave me
    trembling;
As powerful as arrows they strike
    the heart,
    building armored walls that
      keep Love at bay.
They cling like parasites upon their
    host,
    murmuring secretly in the
      darkness,
    "Who can see us?
    Who can cast us out?
We have hidden ourselves well, we
    will hold strong."
    For our inward minds and hearts
    are deep!
Yet the Beloved will root them out
    with Love;
    they will be loosened suddenly.
Because of their insecurity, they will
    run and falter; and
    all who see new life arise
      will wonder.
Then the peoples will be in awe;
    they will tell of all the Beloved
      has done,
    and ponder the power of Love.

Let those who have Awakened rejoice
in the Beloved,
let them celebrate with glad
hearts!
Let all who know Love give witness
to our birthright!

❧

Psalm 65

Praise belongs to You, O Indwelling
Beloved, and
to You we commit our lives,
to You who hear our prayers!
To You we come when we go astray;
When our transgressions fill us
with guilt,
You do forgive us.
Blessed are those who draw near
to You,
those who dwell in your Heart!
Awaken us to your kindness,
enter into the Sacred Chapel
of our heart!

Through pain and suffering, your
Presence sustains us,
O Merciful One, our Comforter,
You, the hope of all the earth to
the distant shore that brings us Home.

By your Light the foundations were
        created being guided by Love;
You still the roaring of the
                seas,
        the pounding of waves,
        the tumult of the peoples,
So that those who dwell even at
                earth's outer bounds
        recognize and reverence You.
At the rise of each morning, and
        as the sun sets at night,
        the people bow their heads
                in reverent gratitude.

You visited the earth and slaked
                our thirst,
        offering Living Streams of
                water;
        You fed the hungry,
        and taught of Love's way.
You watered hardened souls,
        filled with stone and weeds,
        softening them with kindness,
                and blessing their growth.
You crowned your years with
                abandonment,
        inviting all to Eternal Life.
In the desert flowers come forth,
        the pastures flourish with
                fruit and grain;
        Creation's diversity is glorious!
May all people honor these gifts
                with joyful song
        while walking the path of Love.

Psalm 66

Sing a joyful song to the Beloved
        all the earth,
     and praise Love's name;
     Sing in glorious exultation!
We say to You, "How magnificent are
        your ways:
So great is your power that fear and
        doubt vanish before You;
You are our Teacher for all ages:
     We, who choose to listen and learn,
        sing songs of gratitude and joy.

Come and see what the Beloved has done;
     wondrous are the deeds of Love.
Remember when the sea turned to
        dry land?
There, we did rejoice in the One,
     who rules by the mighty Spirit
        of Love forever,
Whose eyes keep watch on the
        nations—
     let not those who strive for
        power exalt themselves!

Bless the Beloved, Heart of our hearts,
     let the sound of our praises
        be heard.
You keep us attuned to life and
     guide our feet on solid ground.
For You, O Love, have tested us;
     You have tried us as silver is
        tried.

You have allowed us to fall into
the net;
You have watched us reap all that
we have sown;
we went through fire and
through water,
Yet You have brought us through our
pain and
into your dwelling place.
I enter your Heart surrendered
to Love;
I commend my soul into your
keeping;
all that my lips uttered, all that
my mouth promised when
I was in trouble and pain,
I offer up to You;
I abandon myself into your hands.

Come and hear, all you who reverence
the Most High,
and I shall tell what the Beloved
has done for me.
I cried aloud to the Silent Watcher
of my life;
from my tongue came forth words
of praise.
Had I cherished greed and power,
I would have separated myself
from Love;
the voice of my prayer was heard.

Blessed be the holy Name of the Beloved,
Loving Companion Presence,
who embraced me, and renewed
my life.

Psalm 67

The Beloved is gracious to us,
 a loving Presence within us;
 The Radiant One shines in us.
O, that Love's Way would be lived
  throughout the earth,
 Love's abiding power embraced
 by all the nations.
May the people ever rejoice in You
 singing songs of appreciation
  for all that You, O Beloved,
  freely give to us.

Let the nations listen and heed;
 we are all called to live with
  integrity and justice.
For You, O Blessed Counselor, will
 guide every nation on earth
 as the leaders and people open
  their hearts and respond.

Abandoning ourselves into the
  Heart of Love,
 we need not worry or fret; for
Love's grace abides wherever we are.
 In Love let us make our home.

Psalm 68

Impregnate us with Love, O Comforter!
Let our fears be transformed;
let all that keeps us separated
and confused flee!
As smoke is blown away, so let our
fears rise up before You;
as wax melts before fire,
let our fears be melted by Love!
Then will we be released
from bondage;
we will exult before the Beloved;
we will be jubilant with joy!

Sing to the Beloved, the Name above
all names;
lift up a song to our Blessed Friend;
commit yourself to loving Service!

Merciful to the poor and kind to
the lowly
is the Comforter, who dwells within.
With compassion are the desolate
given a home,
the prisoners set free;
But those who run from Love live
in a parched land.

O Beloved, reach into the hearts
of your people,
enter into the darkness of
their fears;
As the earth quakes, as floods strike
without warning,
your Presence is within us.

As the mountains tremble and volcanoes
        spew forth ash,
     your Presence is within us.
As rain falls in abundance on
        desert floors,
     restore the lands that they
        might flourish,
     that the flocks may roam and graze
        on fertile fields.
In your Mercy, O Beloved,
      You provide for the needy,
        for those in peril,
        You are with us always.

A new dawn is rising;
      great will be the understanding
        of those who know Love;
The darkness of ignorance will
        be overcome!
The nations will be united in
        their diversity,
      living in harmony and with
        integrity—
Like the wings of a dove covered
        with silver,
      its pinions with gold.
Then will fear be no more,
      Love will reign in every heart!

O mighty mountain, mountain of
        the Most High,
      O Crystal City of the
        New Jerusalem!
Call your people home, out of the
        rubble of this dark age.

Who will rise up to the Heart
of all hearts?
Who will dwell with the Beloved
forever?

A mighty throng will awaken,
millions upon millions,
to the Beloved who dwells within,
They will hear with the heart's ear,
with their heart's eye will
they see.
Even many who knew not Love
will come into the Light.

Blessed be the Beloved,
who daily bears us up,
the Comforter who leads us
to wholeness.
The Beloved calls us to new life,
and guides our feet away
from darkness.

Yes, the Beloved will empower us
with love,
as we face the fears within.
Love ever whispers, "I will break
down the walls of illusion,
I will shatter the fears
that bind,
That you may walk in a new dawn,
that you may dance with
light hearts
and spread peace throughout
the earth."

Then will there be a great celebration,
        O Beloved,
    as the peoples come into the
        Light—
The singers in front, the musicians
        will follow,
    children will join the
        procession:
"Bless the Beloved before the
        peoples,
    the Holy One, the Giver
        of Life!"
All nations will partake in this
        new Life,
    from the East and the West,
    from the North and the South,
        will the peoples come.

Call forth our strength, O Beloved;
    stand by us as we break down
        the fears that bind us.
Because You dwell in our hearts,
    we are strong and live
        with courage.
We shall walk among the beasts
    that dwell among the weeds,
    the doubts that weaken and
        confuse us.
We shall root our fears out of
        the darkness
    with beams of your Love.
Let all within that separate us
        beware,
    as we stretch out our hands
        to the Beloved.

Sing to the Beloved, O nations
of the earth;
sing praises to the One
who is Love,
To the One who gathers the nations
together, to the Beloved,
whose voice is heard in the
Silence.
Ascribe wisdom to the Indwelling Presence,
who invites us to understanding,
and calls us to live in peace.
Majestic is Love in our hearts,
the Beloved, Heart of our heart,
who gives strength and wisdom
to the people.
Blessed be the Beloved!

Psalm 69

Come to my aid, O Beloved!
For my fears threaten to drown me.
I sink in the mire of confusion,
where there is no foothold;
I have entered deep waters,
and the flood sweeps over me.
I am exhausted from weeping;
I thirst as in a desert.
I no longer see the path while
waiting for your return.

More in number than the hairs
          of my head
        are the fears that I carry;
So mighty are they, the walls that
          I built
        can no longer withstand them.
What must I do, O Merciful One,
        to be at peace once again?
O, Life of my life, You know my pretenses,
        the wrongs I have done are not
            hidden from You.

Let those who search for You
        not use me as a guide,
            O Heart of all hearts;
Let those who seek to do your Will
        abandon themselves into your
            keeping, O Loving Counselor.
For in turning from You have I borne
            the consequences, so
        that doubt and loneliness now
            companion me.
I have become as a stranger in my
            own home,
        an alien to my inner being.

O, that zeal for your Truth might
            consume me,
        that persecutions assailing me
            might be for your sake.
Let me humble my soul with mind-
            fasting;
        O Beloved, create within me a
            clean heart!

Let me live simply, sharing what I have
            with those in need,
        that the abundance of your creation
            might be reflected!
Let me speak out of the Silence,
        that through the words given,
        others will learn of You!

Come to my aid, Gentle Healer, for
            my prayer is to You.
In your perfect timing, Beloved,
        in the abundance of your Love,
            answer my cry.
With your strength, O Rock, lift me up,
        let me not sink into the mire;
Let me be delivered from my fears
            as from deep waters.
Let not the flood sweep over me,
        or the deep swallow me up, or
            the abyss overwhelm me.

Answer me, O Beloved, for I know of
            your compassion;
        in your abundant mercy, turn
            toward me.
Do not hide yourself from your
            wayward child.
Draw near to me as in days gone by,
            redeem me,
        set me free from my fears as
        I repent of my erring ways.

For You know how I have strayed,
        You know my feelings of guilt
            and my regret;
        my fears also are known to You.

How small I feel when I turn to You;
You who were insulted and spit upon,
whose Heart was pierced with
no one to comfort You.
They gave You no food of understanding,
and for your thirst, they gave
You vinegar to drink.

Let me come once again to your Table,
Beloved,
forgive all that separates me
from You,
that I might be made whole.
Let me see with the heart's eye;
let me hear through the heart's ear.
Give me the sensitivity to hear
your Word,
and the courage to speak it.
May my home become a house of prayer,
that others might come to bask
in your Presence.
May those who have been oppressed
and persecuted
come and find safety and solace
within its doors.

Increase my faith as You draw near,
Loving Companion Presence.
May many come to know You within
their hearts!
Surprise them with the Spirit of Joy,
that they might be glad and
rejoice!

Take heed of my affliction and pain;
let your saving grace, O Beloved,
set me on high!

I will praise your Name with song;
    I will magnify You with
        thanksgiving.
For I know this pleases You more
        that complaints, or
    false promises made under duress.
Let the oppressed see and be glad;
    you who seek the Beloved,
    let your hearts be renewed.
For the Heart of all hearts hears
        those in need,
    and pours out Compassion to
        those in bondage.

Let heaven and earth praise the Creator,
    the seas and all that dwell
        therein.
For in the Most High lies our salvation,
    the healing of the nations;
And we, the people of the Eternal One,
        are invited, we are called,
    to co-creation, to co-operation;
    thus will future generations inherit
        the planet renewed,
    and those who live the way of Love
        shall dwell with Love forever.
        Amen.

Psalm 70

You take delight, O Radiant One,
  in gracing me with new life!
O Beloved, come and renew me!
Let me face my weaknesses and all
   that confuses me,
  that keeps me from joy!
I seek forgiveness for my
   wrongdoings,
  I desire only You!
Let me begin anew, as a child
   at its mother's breast,
  who basks in love.

May all who seek You
  rejoice and be glad!
May all who surrender to You
   cry out,
  "My joy is in the Beloved!"
Yes, when I am lowly and fear-filled;
  You hasten to me, Beloved!
You are my strength and my joy;
  O Love, come and renew me again!

Psalm 71

In You, O my Beloved, do I
   take refuge;
Let me never feel separated
   from You!
In your compassion come and
   refresh me;
  listen to my cry,
  answer my plea!
Be to me a rock, a tower
   of strength,
  a strong arm to uphold me,
  as I abandon myself into
   your hands.

Be a very Presence to me as
   fear grips me,
  as I grow old and my friends
   leave me.
For You, O Friend, are my hope,
  my strength, since I was
   but a child.
Upon You have I trusted from
   my birth,
  You, whom I knew before
   my mother's womb.
I continually sing praises to You!

I have been a burden to many; now
  in You alone will I trust.
I am filled with gratitude and
  sing your praises all the day.

Do not abandon me in my old age;
    desert me not when my strength
        is spent, or
    when my mind plays tricks
        with me.
For fears rise up to confuse me,
    doubts and forgetfulness
        band together,
And say, "the Beloved no longer
        dwells with you;
    there is no one to stand by you."

O Friend, be not far from me;
    O Beloved, come and enfold me
        in your Presence!
Help me to release my fears.
    Hear my prayer that these fears
        may be transformed,
    O You, who are my Counselor.

As I surrender myself into your
        hands,
    I praise You more and more.
I tell others of your goodness,
    of your compassion and grace
        all the day;
    for your glory is beyond my
        understanding.
As I grow in inner peace and
        serenity,
    I sing songs of thanksgiving
        to You, my Friend!

You who have done wondrous things,
    O Beloved, who is like You?

You who have seen me through
                many fears,
          strengthen me again;
From the depths of despair
          You renew my spirit,
You increase my trust, and You
                comfort me.

I praise you in the Silence
                of my heart,
          for your steadfast Love,
                O my Beloved!
I offer my prayers out to others,
          extending your Love.
My heart leaps for joy, as
          I whisper to You in
                the night—
          my soul also, which You renew
                within me is also glad.

And I tell my friends as well as
                strangers
          of your abounding grace and
                kindness.
For my fears have diminished,
          my strength has returned;
          I will live my remaining years
                in peace.
Blessed be the Beloved, who dwells
                in all hearts!

Psalm 72

Bring justice to the peoples,
            O Beloved,
        and your mercy to all
            generations!
May the people be known for
            mercy,
        rendering justice to the poor!
Let their spirits soar as the eagle,
        let joy abide in every heart!
May we heed the cry of the poor—
            the young and the old,
        helping to free all those in need,
        awakening the souls of oppressors!

May we know oneness with You
            as long as the sun endures,
        as long as the stars shine,
        throughout all generations!
May we acknowledge You in the rain
            falling on the fields,
        like showers that water the earth!
In our day may justice flourish,
            and peace abound,
        throughout all the nations!

May every heart open to your Love
            from sea to sea,
        from the River of Life out
            to the universe!
May fears that paralyze the people
        rise up from the depths
            into Your Light!

May the leaders of nations from
        all the earth,
      listen to Love's Voice;
May they spend time in Silence
        before they counsel!
May the leaders surrender to
      your Love, and the nations
      serve the Most High!
For You heed the needy when
        they call,
      the poor and those who have
        no friend.
You have compassion on the weak,
        the downtrodden,
      giving them strength and
        hope.
From injustice and oppression,
      You redeem their life;
      and precious are they in
        your Heart.

Long may You live in our hearts,
        may praises be sung to You!
May our prayers rise up before You
      and blessings of love be
        freely rendered!
May we be ever grateful for the
        grain of the fields,
      for the fruits of the vine
        to be shared with all;
And may the people blossom forth
        in the cities, diverse
      like flowers in the meadow!
May your Name live on forever,
      your Love endure as long as
        the sun!

May the people bless themselves
          in knowing You, and
     all nations call You blessed!

Blessed be the Beloved, the One
          who dwells in open hearts,
          who guides us along the way.
Blessed be You, who come in
               Name of Love;
          may your glory fill the earth!
               Amen and Amen!

Psalm 73

Truly the Beloved is near to those
          with open hearts,
     to those who abandon themselves
          to Love.
But as for me, I almost lost
          the way, when
     my heart was consumed with
          my own desires.
For I was arrogant and yearned
          for wealth,
     when I saw the power of
          the rich.

For they seem to have little
          conscience,
     and are appointed well in
          all things.

They can buy their way out of
    trouble,
        and lack for nothing that
            power can buy.
Therefore pride is their necklace;
    greed covers them as a
        garment.
They become puffed up and
    deceitful,
        their heart's ear closed to
            Love's voice.
They speak with contempt for the
    poor, and
        haughtily they threaten
            oppression.
They rationalize their avarice
    believing themselves above
        Love's way.

In turn the people praise them,
    and yearn to follow on
        their path.
And they say, "Because we are
    prosperous,
        we are blessed by the
            Most High;
        surely upright are our ways."
Behold, these are the ignorant;
    always at ease, they increase
        in riches.
Has it been in vain that
    I have opened my heart,
    and washed my hands
        in innocence?

For trouble seems to follow me,
        as I weep over the injustice
        that seems to blanket the world.

If I had pursued their ways,
        I would have been untrue to
                my birthright.
Yet when I tried to understand this,
        it seemed beyond my
                comprehension,
Until I sat in the Silence and
                prayed;
        then a veil lifted and
                I could see.

Truly they walk a dangerous road
        with fear as their constant
                companion.
For when their wealth is lost,
        or disaster threatens to bring
                them down,
They will have forgotten the only
                Treasure,
        they will be so far from their
                true Estate.

When my soul was embittered,
        when I was arrogant at heart,
I was blind and ignorant;
        I was like a spoiled child
                to its parents.
Still You were ever near to me,
        You waited for me to see.
Now You guide me with your
                counsel,
        I am at home in your Heart.

What is my Treasure but your
            Love?
        There is nothing upon earth
        that I desire besides You.
My body and my mind may fail,
        but You are the strength of
            my heart
        and my joy forever.

Those who are far from You will
            live in fear;
        You do not compel them to
            open their hearts.
As for me, I delight in walking
            with the Beloved;
        I invited the Friend into
            my heart,
        that I might live with Love.

Psalm 74

O Beloved of my heart, what does it mean
        that I feel separated from You?
        How is it that I fear your anger
            and condemnation?
I have known your Presence in days
            gone by,
        when You counseled me as a guide
            and a friend.

I remember your Holy Temple,
within my heart.
In your mercy, direct me once again
before fear destroys me and
leads me too far astray!

Doubt and anxiety have crept into the
Inner Tabernacle,
erecting walls as a defense.
My mind dwells on hurts of the past
and foresees a dim future.
All the beauty and joy of companioning
with You
Is lost in the anger that consumes me;
I become a prisoner in my
own being.
I say to myself, "I will subdue these
fears," even knowing that
only your refining Fire will
rout them out.

I do not know my inner self;
how long must I walk alone?
Like many, will I fear crying out
to the One, who knows all hearts?
How long, O Beloved, will fear laugh
at my folly?
Will it keep me bound forever?
In your mercy, direct me once again,
before fear destroys me and
leads me too far astray!

You have companioned us forever,
working salvation in the midst
of our humanity.

You fashion us together even as
        we seek to destroy one another;
        You are our Rock as we face
                the demons within.
You forgive us when we are
                contrite, and
        nourish our souls in the
                wilderness.
You are the Living Water assuaging
                our thirst,
        a comfort in our desert days,
                our barren ways.
        Who is like You?
Yours is the day, yours also the
                night;
All suns and galaxies are established
                by Love Consciousness.
You created the boundaries of the
                world;
        the seasons belong to You.

When I call upon You, O Beloved,
                pride and arrogance flee,
        and your strength upholds me.
You revive my spirit, and I live
                in peace; for
        You are with the poor in spirit
                forever.

I shall always remember your covenant,
        as the shadows within rise up
                to the Light.
Love will stand by as these fears
                are released;
        in the Silence where we meet,
                I shall praise your Name!

Come, O Beloved, counsel me with love;
In your mercy, direct me once again
before fear destroys me and
leads me too far astray!
O Companioning Presence, make your
Home in my heart.

Psalm 75

I yearn to know You, O Beloved,
to abide in the Peace of Love;
I choose to turn from the ways
of the world, where
ego separates and divides.

"At the set time which I appoint,
I will judge with equity.
When the earth totters with
all its inhabitants,
it is I who keep steady
its axis."
I say to the powerful,
"Lead with justice and mercy."
And to the greedy,
"Share your abundance with
those in need.
Let no one see your acts of mercy,
or know your works of
charity."

For not from the four directions,
      nor from the heights or the
          depths comes lifting up;
Rather, it is the Most High who
        fulfills the balance,
      sifting as a Thresher,
      burning as a refining Fire.
For hidden within the heart of
        each soul,
      there dwells the Divine Guest,
      that knows well our secret
        thoughts,
      that weighs us in the balance.

Let us rejoice and be glad!
      Let us sing praises to the
        Beloved!
As the unjust and oppressors dwell
        in the wilderness,
      those who live with mercy and truth
      will soar like the eagle.

Psalm 76

*I*n loving places, O Beloved,
      are You known,
     your mercy extends to all
      the earth.

Your abode has been established
in our soul,
your dwelling place in our heart.
You break down our walls—
our anger, fear, illusions
and doubts.
Glorious are You, more majestic
than the everlasting mountains.
That which is haughty within us
is brought low,
our greed brings us to ruin;
The violence that we harbor
turns in upon ourselves.
In your loving mercy, O Beloved,
You raise us up with Love.

For You fill us with wonder!
You, who know our innermost
being,
You forgive us and raise us up.
From the depths of our soul
You call us to Awaken,
to grow toward harmony
and wholeness.
You well up in our hearts with
the inward call
to liberate the oppressed
of the earth.

Surely our fear-filled hearts will
one day praise You,
the gold that comes out of
the ashes of our ego.
Abandon yourself to the Beloved
with confidence; and

receive the blessings of Love
from the Heart of your heart,
From the One who yearns for
your return,
Who welcomes you Home with joy!

Psalm 77

I cry aloud to You, O Friend,
to the Eternal Listener, that
I might be heard.
In the day of trouble I seek the
Beloved;
in the night my hand is
stretched out in prayer;
my soul yearns to be comforted.

I think of the Beloved, and I moan;
I meditate, and my spirit
is weak.
You trouble me and I cannot
find peace;
I am so fearful,
I cannot sleep;
I am so filled with fantasies
I cannot speak out.
How well I remember years past,
when You were a companion
close by.

I commune with my heart all
through the night;
I meditate, my spirit seeking
its Friend:
"Will You abandon me forever, and
leave me comfortless in my
distress?
Where is your steadfast Love that
made my soul to sing?
Are your promises empty, that
I feel so alone?"

"Where is the Comforter to ease
this emptiness?
How have I offended You, O Friend,
that I am so alone?"
And I wonder, "Is it those walls of
fear and guilt,
that separate me from the very
Heart of my heart?"

I call to mind the closeness of
my Friend;
yes, I remember the joy of
the Beloved's presence.
I contemplate in the Silence,
recalling how You led me
along the Way;
For your Way, O Beloved, is holy.
There is no other like You!
You are the One who will bring
us to wholeness,
You manifest your Love to all
who call upon You;

With You the peoples are redeemed,
    the nations brought to peace.

When our fears sense You, O Beloved,
    when our doubts encounter
        your Love,
    they are afraid and attack.
Our eyes pour forth oceans of tears;
    our countenance grows cloudy;
    we hide behind walls of
        resistance.

The power of your Love seems
        too much for us;
    your Light unveils the secrets
        hidden in our heart;
    Can You wonder that we tremble?
Yet, You stand beside us as we walk
        through our fears to
    the path of wholeness and love,
    though our footsteps are unsure.
You send the Counselor as a guide
    to lead us on the road to peace,
    truth, and love.

Psalm 78

Listen well, O peoples of the earth,
          to inner promptings of the Spirit;
Let Silence enter your house that
               you may hear!
For within your heart Love speaks:
          not with words of deceit,
But of spiritual truths to guide you
               upon the paths of peace.
Do not hide this from your children;
          teach of the inward Voice, and
          help all generations to listen
               in the Silence,
That they may know the Beloved and
               be free
          to follow the precepts of Love.

For the Spirit of Truth is written
               upon open hearts, that
          we might share the Divine Plan,
And model to the children Love's way
               as we have been shown;
That each new generation might honor
               Silence,
          the children yet unborn.
Herein lies the hope of the future:
          to live as co-creators with
               the great Creator,
          Not like those who live in
               ignorance
          too impatient to wait for Love's word,
Whose spirits are not faithful to their
               birthright of Love.

Since the birth of consciousness,
  armed with free will,
    many there are who have rebelled
    against the Creator.
They did not keep the great Covenant
    but refused to live according to
      Love's way.
They forgot their purpose and the
      beautiful Plan,
    and all that had been given
      as Gift.
Throughout the ages, the Eternal Lover
    has shown the marvels of Creation,
      wonders to behold.

Remember how the sea was divided so
    the people passed through,
    how the waters stood as a wall;
How in the daytime, they were led
      with a cloud,
    and through the night with a
      fiery light.
Recall how the rocks in the wilderness
      cracked open,
    that the people might drink their
      fill as from the deep;
Yes, streams came out of the rock,
    and caused waters to flow down
      like rivers.

Yet did the people close their hearts,
    rebelling against the Most High,
      living in a wilderness.
Over and over, they tested Love
    by demanding that their desires
      be met.

Speaking against Love, they cried,
    "Can the Mighty One not spread
      a feast for us?
The rocks opened so that water
      gushed out
    and streams overflowed.
Can we not also expect bread and meat
      to be provided for us?"

Did they not know how their rebellions
    separated them from the Source
      of all that is?
How often the people lost faith
      on the journey,
    not trusting in the saving power
      of the Beloved!
Even so, their complaints were answered
      with compassion;
And the doors to heaven opened
    raining down their sustenance,
      the very grain of heaven.
They ate of the bread of the angels;
    food was sent in abundance.

The East wind blew in the heavens,
    and the South wind was
      called forth;
Out of heaven's abundance came the
      winged birds,
    as many as the sand of the seas;
They fell right in their midst,
    all around their habitation,
And the people ate and were well filled;
    all that they craved was given
      to them.

Yet justice prevailed, retribution
was made,
even as their mouths were still
filled with food.
To restore the balance, the strongest
among them died,
the strongest in their midst.

In spite of all this, the people
continued to separate themselves
from Love;
their eyes and ears were closed.
So they lived their days in fear,
and their years in terror.
When they fell, they sought the Most High;
they repented and sought help
earnestly.
They remembered then the Rock,
who was their strength,
the Almighty One, their Redeemer.
Flattery poured from their mouths,
lies issued from their tongues.
Their hearts were not filled with love;
they were not true to the covenant.
Still the Beloved, being compassionate,
forgave their hypocrisy and
gave them new life.
How patient was the Eternal Lover,
how blind to their fickle hearts,
Knowing that they believed themselves
to be but flesh,
a wind that passes and comes
not again.
How often the people rebelled against Love
in the wilderness,

grieving the Beloved with their
distance!

How often they tested Love and turned
their backs to the Holy One!
They forgot the power of Love, and
the times that they were saved,
When they were comforted by signs,
and sustained through miracles.
Through all generations the rivers
have flowed,
rivers now polluted by greed.
Through famine and floods, the Beloved
has brought forth new life.
All through the ages, the earth has
yielded its bountiful harvest;
yet, valleys and mountains, forests
and fields have been misused.
Yes, greed has become the great
destroyer of life,
taking without offering back,
consuming the earth with abandon,
leaving death, disease, and destruction
in its wake.
We cannot be spared what we have sown;
Generations to come will suffer from
our willful ways;
their lives will be a mirror to blind
and stubborn hearts.
Injustice, oppression, and greed will turn
back upon hearts of stone;
children unborn will reap a harvest
of lost dreams.
Even so, the Source of all life remains
faithful,

ever-ready to lead us out of the
wilderness,
to speak to us in the Silence of
our hearts.
Yes, You are our hope, our strength, and
our comfort;
our fears will not overwhelm us.
You will guide us to the New Jerusalem,
to the Mountain of Hope, the
City of Light!
You will be an ever-living Presence
to those who call upon your Name,
to all who open their hearts
to Love.
When, O peoples of the earth, will you
stop testing and rebelling against
the Source of Life?
When will you awaken and live
according to Love,
And attune yourselves to the music
of the spheres?
For as you turn back to the Beloved,
listening for Love's voice within
your own heart,
you will live with integrity,
you will radiate love.
When you call upon the Beloved,
your prayers will be heard;
your needs will be met
abundantly.
The Beloved is a stranger to those
who choose to walk in darkness,
to all who are the enemies of Light.
For You, Love of all loves, gift us
with freedom

to follow the way of Life, or
to live in the shadow of death.
Who will awaken our sleeping minds,
and lift up our hearts to
the Truth?
Who will rouse us from apathy,
quicken our spirits that we might
serve your Plan?
The Beloved awaits our response to
the new dawn,
where the people of earth will be
united in peace,
Where harmony will reign forever in
the beauty of diversity, and
all nations will bow before
the Most High.

Those who choose the way of darkness,
who follow the road of ignorance,
become lost;
They know not the joy of abandonment
to Love's Companioning Presence.
O peoples of Earth, O nations around
the globe,
turn back to Love, build anew upon
strong foundations,
renew your commitment to the
Divine Plan!
Listen long in the Silence that the Word
may be heard,
that decisions arise from the depths
of your Inner Being where
Wisdom dwells.
For the Spirit of Trugh is written upon
gentle and open hearts,
not as on stones of old.

With steadfast love, will the Counselor
                guide you; and
        to all who abandon themselves to
            the Beloved
        will the Divine Plan be revealed.
                Amen and amen!

Psalm 79

O Merciful Presence, the ignorant seem
                unrestrained in the world;
        they defile the Sacred Altar, your
                dwelling place within;
        they leave those weaker than themselves
                in ruins.
Chaos and destruction follow them, as
        they oppress the poor through
                deception and greed, and
        kill the faith-filled who resist.
Yes, they have poured out their blood
                like water throughout the world;
        many have disappeared without a trace.
How long will the unjust bring anguish
                to the loving, to those
        who seek justice and peace?

How long, O Indwelling Presence?
        Will your patience last forever?
        When will You awaken our long
                dormant spirits?

Pour out your Love on every nation,
    open the hearts of all people;
We await a new birth of Consciousness,
    we call upon your Name!
For the ignorant and unloving are laying
    waste to the planet.

Forgive us for the misuse and abuse
    of your Creation;
       humble us with your steadfast Love,
       before the world becomes a barren
       waste.
Help us, O Compassionate One, to renew
    the face of the earth;
       deliver us, and forgive our sins,
       that we might know the joy of
       co-creation!
Let other nations not cry out,
    "Where is their faith?"
Let all who have spilled the blood
    of the innocent
       repent and make reparation before
       the eyes of the world!

Let the cries of the victims of injustice
    come before You;
       according to your great Power,
       break the bonds of oppression!
Let all that has been garnered through
    greed
       be returned in full measure with
       open hands.
Then we your people, those who would
    companion with You,
       will give thanks to You forever;

from generation to generation we will
abandon ourselves into your hands
with grace-filled, open hearts.

Psalm 80

*E*ternal Listener, give heed to
your people,
You, who are our Guide and our
Light!
You, who dwell amidst the angels,
shine forth into the heart of
all nations!
Enliven your people with compassion
that peace and justice
might flourish.

Restore us, O Holy One;
let your face shine upon us,
teach us to love!

Gentle Teacher, help us to turn
to You in prayer,
fasting from our negative thoughts.
In your steadfast Love, You weep
with our tears,
tears that rise from fear,
doubt, and illusion.

You uphold us when we feel the sting
of pride,
when our anxiety threatens to
paralyze us.

Restore us, O Holy One;
let your face shine upon us,
teach us to love!

You companion us through the wilderness,
through the shadows created by fear.
You plant your Seed into each heart.
You uproot the weeds of our sin,
You cultivate the soil of our
goodness.
Truly, in You, we become like a tiny
acorn,
holding the secret of a mighty oak.
You nourish us with the food of Love,
with streams of Living Water.
Be our strength as we break down walls
that separate and divide;
let not fear pluck away the gifts
we would share.
Roll away the stones that become obstacles
to growth,
to producing a bountiful harvest.

Receive our gratitude, O Heart of
all hearts!
Look upon us and see what
Love can do;
rejoice in the new birth
that You create!

Be glad where your Seed has found
fertile soil.
How much more the return of one
healthy plant
than ten thousand useless weeds!
May those who have borne the fruit
of love
radiate your Spirit into the world!
May we always walk and co-create
with You;
receive the gratitude of our hearts,
as we share in the Great Plan!

Restore us, O Holy One!
Let your face shine upon us,
teach us to love!

Psalm 81

Sing in unison to the Most High,
our strength;
shout for joy and join the
celebration!
Raise a song, sound the great bells,
the flute and the harp.
Blow the trumpet at the new moon,
at the full moon, and on all
the feast days.

Sing in gratitude to the Great Hunter,
  to the One who seeks out
    all hearts.
Give thanks in the congregations that
  the Good News may be heard
    throughout the land.

I hear a Voice I have come to know:
  "I relieve your shoulder of the
    burden;
  your spirit is free to create.
In distress when you call, I come
    to you;
  I answer you in the secret place
    of your heart;
  I invite you to the grace
    of forgiveness.
Hear, O my people, while I caution you!
  O, dear friends, if you would but
    listen!
Do not make of riches and ambition a
    powerful god;
  do not become puffed up with pride
    and arrogance.
I am your very breath; I have been
    with you from the beginning.
  Open your heart wide, and
    I shall fill it."

Who among you will listen to the voice
  of the Beloved?
  How many will open their heart?
All you too stubborn to hear,
  who follow your own counsel,
  will know fear and loneliness.

"Oh that my people would listen,
　　that, as friends, you would
　　　　walk in my ways!
Your fears would soon flee and
　　your hearts would overflow.
You, who turn your backs on Love,
　　will know only momentary pleasure,
　　your reward will soon be spent.
I would satisfy your hunger,
　　and, with streams of Living Water,
　　you would live in the joy
　　　　of heaven here on earth!"

Psalm 82

O Compassionate Teacher, You are our
　　merciful Counselor;
　　in the Silence You make yourself known
　　　　to all who take time to listen.
Would that those in power would heed
　　your Voice:
　　"How long will you misuse power
　　　　that oppresses the poor?
When will you learn that to act
　　justly and with integrity will
　　bring mutual blessing to all?
Do you not know that to give
　　　　succour to the poor
　　and to free people to succeed
　　will bring you more joy than
　　　　All your bank accounts?"

Arise! Awaken to the new dawn!
    Come into the Light; shed darkness
      like skin on the snake!
    For the foundations of the cosmos
      are shaking with injustice.

I say, "Within you dwells the Beloved,
      the Breath of your breath;
Open your heart in the Silence and
    know the One in the many."

Arise! Join in the new creation!
    Let harmony reign among all
      the nations!

Psalm 83

O Great Creator, do not keep silence;
    do not withhold your peace or
      be still, O Giver of Life!
For fear is rampant in the world;
    those who rule by oppression
      rise up with power.
They lay deceptive plans against
    the people;
    they consult together against
      freedom and justice.
Crafty words belie intent as thousands
    reap dire consequence;

nations go to war and the
innocent suffer!
Yes, they conspire with one accord;
against Love they make a
covenant—
No institution is free from the
insidious arm of corruption,
at home and in fields afar.
Who will succor the homeless, the
orphans, the starving,
those cast aside by decisions
based on greed?
Who will speak up on their behalf?
Let all with faith-filled hearts
rise up with Love!

Clothe us in the dress of your peace,
and the stronghold of your mercy,
that we might bear the power
of Love;
Let us walk in shoes of integrity,
and don the mantle of truth.
Let us shed the tatters of envy and
fear,
the rags of anger and greed,
And say, "We shall seek only
the Truth,
which will set us free!"

O Beloved, let all that is unholy
within us be cleansed,
erased as chalk from a slate.
As fire consumes the forest,
as the flame reaches up to the
heavens,

Let the refining Fire of your Love
reach into the hidden places
within open hearts!
Forgive us and let the deep regret
of our souls
rise up as contrite offerings.
Let the people seek your Word,
let the nations turn from
violence and destruction.
Let them know that You alone,
You who reign with Love,
are the Most High over
all the earth!

Psalm 84

How glorious is your dwelling place,
O Blessed Architect
of the universe!
My soul longs, yes, aches for
the abode of the Beloved;
All that is within me sings for joy
to the living Heart of Love!

Even as the sparrow finds a home,
and the swallow a nesting place,
where its young are raised within
your majestic creation,
You invite us to dwell within
your Heart.

Blessed are they whose hearts are filled
with love,
who sing praises to You with
grateful hearts!

Blessed are they who put their strength
in You,
who choose to share the joy and
sorrows of the world.
They do not give way to fear or doubt;
they are quickened by Divine
Light and Power;
they dwell within the peace of
the Most High.
They go from strength to strength and
live with integrity.

O Eternal Lover, hear my prayer;
give ear, O Divine Comforter!
Forgive what is unholy within me;
free me from my illusions!

For a day within the Heart of Love
is more to be desired than
a thousand elsewhere.
I would rather be a servant in your
dwelling place,
than live in riches among
those who know not Love.
For the Beloved is as radiant as the sun,
as strong as a steel shield,
and invites each one to come,
to partake of the Banquet.
Who will accept the goodness of Love?
Who will seek for spiritual
treasure?

O Loving Creator of the universe,
blessed are all who put their
trust in You!
They bless the world.

Psalm 85

O Beloved, how gracious You are
to your people;
You restore their souls time and
time again.
You forgive their distractions when
they wander far from You;
You give them new Life.

Yes, You bless them and raise up
new hope;
You awaken their hearts
to love.

Restore us again, O Spirit of Truth;
burn us with the refining
Fire of Love!
We cannot live separated from You;
cast out the demons of fear,
doubt, and illusion.
Revive us again, we pray; may
your people rejoice in You!

Have compassion on your people,
      O Holy One,
   and grant us your forgiveness.

Listen, O people, in the silent Chapel
      of your heart; and
   the Beloved will speak of
      peace to you,
  to the hidden saints, to all who
      turn their hearts to Love.
Surely new life is at hand for those
      who reverence Love;
   O, that harmony might dwell
      among the nations.

Steadfast love and faithfulness
      will meet;
   righteousness and peace will
      embrace one another.
Wisdom will spring up from the ground
   and truth will look down from
      the sky.
Yes, the Eternal Giver will grant
      what is good,
   and the lands will yield
      abundantly.
Mercy and compassion are Love's way;
   You will guide our footsteps
      upon the path of peace
  as we recognize with open hearts
      that You are our peace.

· 169 ·

Psalm 86

Give ear to my cry, O Comforter,
       and answer me, for
    I am sorely in need of You.
Awaken new life in me, as I yearn
         to do your Will;
      dispel the ignorance of my ways,
         as I put my trust in You.
You are the Beloved; be gracious to me,
        Heart of my heart,
     for with You would I walk all day.
My soul is uplifted, as I abandon
        myself into your hands.
For You are kind and forgiving,
      abounding in steadfast Love to all
       who call upon You.
Give ear to my prayer, Compassionate One;
     listen to my heartfelt plea.
In the time of trouble, I dare to
       call upon You,
     for You hear the cry of those
      in need.

No one is like You, O Mighty One,
     all of creation belongs to You.
All the nations are under your authority
       and, one day,
     they will acknowledge and reverence
       You;
     they will give praise to your Sacred Name.
For You are great; we are awed by the
       wonders of your world,
     You alone are the Most High.

Teach me your ways, Mighty Counselor,
    that I may walk in truth;
      write my name upon your Heart.
I give You thanks, O Beloved,
       with my whole being;
      O, that I might radiate your Light
      forever!
Great is your steadfast Love toward
       those who call upon You;
     You deliver their souls from
      the depths of despair.

O Beloved, numerous fears rise up
       within me;
    like an army they seek to
       overwhelm me, and
    they would keep me in darkness.
Yet You are merciful and gracious,
    ready to forgive and ever
    abounding in steadfast Love
      and faithfulness.
Be present to me and receive my prayer;
    imbue me with strength, and
    help me to release each fear.
Pour forth your Light into my soul,
    that all that is hidden in
      darkness
    may come forth into awareness.
For You, O Beloved, are my Redeemer
     and my Comforter.

Psalm 87

In the heavenly realm stands the
    City of Light;
    the Beloved welcomes all who come
        to its gate,
    all who have surrendered themselves
        to Love.
Glories await you within the citadel,
    within the City of Light.
Among those who enter are the humble
        and kind,
    those who reflect peace and
        radiate integrity,
    those who have faced darkness
        with Love by their side.
Prepare yourselves for the City of Light
        all you who hear;
    for the Most High reigns there
        in glory.
Your name is written in the holy register;
    when you face the Recorder,
    who will blush with regret, and
    who will join the heavenly chorus?

Those who live by the Spirit of Love
    will know joy and harmony in
    the everlasting Dance of the Cosmos!

Psalm 88

O Beloved, Heart of my heart,
    I call to You for help by day;
    I cry out in the night.
Let my prayer come before You,
    bend your ear to my cry!
For my soul is full of troubles,
    and my life seems like dust,
I have fallen into a pit of
        despair;
    I have no strength and
      I feel powerless,
Like one from whom You have turned,
    like the soil people walk upon.
You alone can comfort me in this
      abyss,
    in the darkness of fear.
Separation from You is an agony,
    hopelessness threatens to
      overwhelm me.
Through You alone can I pray for
      my enemies,
    for those who ignore my plight.
I am in a prison, chained by fear;
    I am weary of tears.
Every day I call upon You, O Beloved;
    I lift up my hands in supplication.
Will You raise me from this
      living death?
    Will You mend a broken heart?
Let not your steadfast Love pass
      me by;
    have mercy on me, O Comforter!

Reach your hand into the darkness of
my ego-fears;
by your saving grace, forgive
my unholy ways.

O Merciful Beloved, I cry to You;
each day my prayer comes before
You.
Let not separation keep me from
your Heart;
be my strength as I face the
darkness inside.
Too long have I let fear control me,
projecting onto others the demons
dwelling within.
Let your Love encircle and envelop me;
in your mercy raise me up.
Let peace become my companion all day
long; by night
free me from the bonds of fear.
Let me be reconciled with family and
friends; and may I know You,
O Loving Companion Presence,
as in days of old.
Amen.

Psalm 89

I will sing of your steadfast Love
        forever, my Beloved;
    with forthright voice I will proclaim
        your goodness to all generations.
For your abiding Love rules the universe,
    your faithfulness extends throughout
        the firmament.
Your Covenant from the beginning of time
    encompasses all who choose to walk
        the path of Love;
And to all generations that honor
        your Way and your Truth,
    will Love make Itself known.

Let the heavens praise your wonders,
        O Loving Creator,
    your faithfulness in the congregation
        of the holy ones!
For who in the universe is comparable
        to You?
    Who among the heavenly beings
        is like You—
You, who are reverenced in the council
        of the holy ones,
    great in wisdom, gentle of heart, and
        one with all around You.
O Most High, mighty are You,
    whose Grace is poured forth
        throughout all ages.
You have blessed us with oceans,
        rivers, and lakes,
    to sustain our life on Earth.

Yes, You entrusted the waters into
our keeping,
and in our stewardship we failed.
Forgive us, O Merciful One.
The heavens are yours, the earth also
belongs to You.
Yet we befoul the air and rape
the earth.
Forgive us, O Merciful One.
The north and south, You have
created them;
the east and the west as well.
With the might of arms, we shatter
the nations,
and scatter your people.
Forgive us, O Merciful One.
Righteousness and justice are the
foundation of the Cosmos;
steadfast love and faithfulness
go before You.
Blessed are those who know your Love,
who walk in the Light of
your countenance!
Blessed are those who call upon
your Name
and extol truth and justice!
For You are the glory of their strength;
You give wise counsel.
Our very lives belong to You,
O Loving Companion Presence!

You have made yourself known to the
faith-filled;
You set them on the path of peace.
The Gift You sent to teach us Love
invites us to eternal life!

Through the Heart of all hearts,
     You opened the way to Life.
Your steadfast Love came among us
       giving us strength.
Fear shall not overcome us,
    we will not give in to doubt.
For your Love casts out our fear
     and gives rise to forgiveness of
       those who would do us wrong.
Yes, your faithfulness and your abiding
      Love are with us,
     and in your Name we can do
     all good things.
Through You is our purpose
     made known,
    that we might know your Will
    and make it our own.
In our gratitude we cry out, "You are
     the Beloved,
    the Most High, our very Breath."
Through You we are born anew,
    the Spirit of Truth comes to us.
Your enduring love is with us forever,
     and your Covenant stands firm
      throughout eternity.
We will know You as Loving Companion
     Presence now
   and in the life to come.

"If your children turn their backs
    and follow not Love's way,
If they oppress the weak and
      befriend injustice,
They will separate themselves from
     Love,
    and they will dwell with fear.

Even so, my steadfast Love will await
                their return,
        my faithfulness will remain sure.
My Covenant stands true forever, as
                does the Life that begets life.
You are all invited to holiness,
        to come to the fulness of
                your birthright.
For Love shall endure forever, and
        Light as the sun before us.
Like the stars, they shall be established
                forever;
        they shall stand true while the
                firmament remains."

So often, You seem cast off and
                rejected, as we
        your people separate ourselves
                from Love.
We renounce the Covenant made with You;
        we choose the ego's fear-filled way.
We build walls to defend ourselves,
        walls that lead to loneliness.
The world is rampant with violence,
        neighbors striving to outdo one
                another.
The nations compete for worldly riches,
        oppressing the weak with deceitful
                promises.
Yes, when we turn our backs on Love,
        we become deaf to the Word
                longing to be heard.
We live according to the gratification
                of our senses,
        forgetting the Treasure hidden in
                the Silence of our hearts.

Be merciful to us, O Holy One, melt
                our hearts of ice
        before the hour of reckoning
                comes upon us!
How long, O people of Earth, will you
                hide yourselves from Love?
        How long will your self-centered ways
                keep you fearful and living
                        in darkness?
Remember, O friends, the values that
                are eternal;
        for vanity withers the soul as
                a husk of corn dying in autumn.
Who will come to the Banquet, the feast
                of heaven here on Earth?
        Who will abandon themselves into
                the hands of Love?

O Beloved, your steadfast Love remains,
                sure and faithful,
        Your promises endure forever.
Awaken us, O Holy One! And humble us
        so we are compelled to cry out
                for forgiveness.
        In your mercy, help us to release
                the fears that veil your Light!
For You alone are the Holy One; You alone
                are our loving Creator.
        Let all who would be free from fear
                commend their lives into
                        your Hands.

Blessed are You, O Loving Companion Presence,
                for ever and ever!
                Amen.

Psalm 90

Eternal and Immortal One, You have been
 our refuge in all generations.
Before the mountains were brought forth,
 before You had formed the earth and
 the world, from
 everlasting to everlasting,
You are the Alpha and the Omega.

When our days on Earth are ended,
 You welcome us home to your Heart,
 to the City of Light,
 where time is eternal
and days are not numbered.

You gather those who love You as
 friends returning from a long
 journey,
 giving rest to their souls.
You anoint them with the balm of
 understanding,
 healing wounds of the past.

For our days on Earth are a mystery,
 a searching for You,
 a yearning for the great Mystery
 to make itself known.
The years pass and soon the
 Harvest is at hand,
 a time to reap the fruit of
 one's life.
Who has lived with integrity?
 Who will reflect the Light
 Who can bear the radiant beams
 of Love?

Who have reverenced the Counselor,
and opened their hearts to the
Spirit of Truth?
Teach us, O Beloved, to honor each day
that we may have a heart
of wisdom.

Awaken us, O Holy One! Too long
have we been asleep!
Have mercy on your people!
Help us to wait in Silence listening
for your gentle Voice;
Strengthen us with courage to
face the fears within.
O, that we might be converted in
our hearts
and walk together in peace and
harmony!
Let your Love be known to the nations,
your Glory to our children's
children.
Let the grace and gentleness of the
Holy Spirit be upon us,
guiding our feet upon paths
of Love Consciousness
Increase the Light within us—
O Beloved, hear our prayer!
Amen.

Psalm 91

Those who dwell in the shelter of
             Infinite Light,
      who abide in the wings of
             Infinite Love,
Will raise their voices in praise:
      "My refuge and my strength;
      in You alone will I trust."
For You deliver me from the webs
             of fear and illusion,
      from all that separates and divides;
You protect me as an eagle shields
             its young,
      Your faithfulness is sure, like
             an arrow set upon the mark.
I will not fear the shadows of the night,
      nor the confusion that comes
             by day,
Nor the dreams that awaken me from
             sleep,
      nor the daily changes that
             life brings.

Though a thousand may deride this
             radical trust,
      ten thousand laugh as I seek
             to do your Will,
Yet will I surrender myself to You,
      abandoning myself into your Hands
      without reserve.

For You have sent your angels to
             watch over me,
      to guide me in all my ways.

———————

On their hands, they will bear me up,
      lest I dash my foot against
          a stone.
Though I walk among those who
          roar like a lion,
      or are as stealthy as the adder,
      in your strength will I endure.

"Because you cleave to Me in love,
          I will deliver you;
      I will protect you, who
          call upon my Name.
When you call to Me, I will answer you;
      I will be with you in times
          of trouble,
      I will rescue you so that
          you will know my Peace,
All through the years, will I dwell
          in your heart,
      as Loving Companion Presence,
          forever."

Psalm 92

It is good to give thanks to You,
      O Beloved, to sing
    praises to your Holy Name,

To affirm your gracious Love
in the morning,
and your faithfulness through
the night,
To the music of the spheres,
to the melody of the universe!
For You, Heart of my heart, gladden
my soul,
as I proclaim with joy the harmony
and beauty of creation.

How wondrous is your Divine Plan,
O Beloved,
Your design, brought forth by Love!
The ignorant cannot perceive,
those who still sleep cannot
understand:
Though darkness covers much of
the land
and violence seems to flourish,
Love gives birth to dazzling Light,
and, like a laser,
it shines through to all that
is hidden.
Yet, lo, all those who separate
themselves from Love,
will be undone by fear.

You delight in my spirit and elevate
my soul;
You bathe me in the oil of
kindness.
My eyes behold the radiance of
creation's glory,
my ears echo with Love's refrain.

Those who live with integrity are like
a garden in full bloom,
whose blossoms beautify the earth.
They are planted in the dwelling place
of Love,
their produce nourishes all those
who pass by.
All through their lives they reap
bountiful harvests,
overflowing as a cornucopia of
the finest fruits,
Magnifying the Blessed Gardener,
living as sons and daughters
of the Most High.

Psalm 93

The Almighty reigns adorned in majesty;
the Creator is robed and girded
with strength.
Yes, the world is established and
given into our care;
our stewardship of the earth reflects
our love for You,
You, who are and ever shall be.

The cosmos celebrates your goodness,
O Beloved,
the waters lift up their voice,
the winds speak through their roaring.

Mightier than the thunder of
　　　　many storms,
　　　mightier than the waves of the sea,
　　　　is the Heart of Love!

That which you ordain is certain;
　　　holiness befits your house,
　　　our hearts, your dwelling place,
　　　　O Beloved, for evermore.

Psalm 94

O Heart of Pure Fire, You who
　　　cleanse and refine us,
　　Compassionate One, shine forth!
In your mercy, rise up and
　　　Awaken those who still sleep
　　　　in ignorance!
O Heart of all hearts, break open
　　　the hearts of your people,
　　that we might hear your Voice
　　　and heed your Word!

Too often we spew forth arrogant words,
　　we boast with heads held high.
We oppress the weak in our blindness,
　　and turn a deaf ear to the cries
　　　of the poor.

We ignore the lonely and turn aside
        from the stranger,
    too many children go hungry to bed.
And, we think, "This is not our concern;
    let them pray to God for help!"

Understand, O dullest of the people!
        When will the ignorant Awaken?
The Beloved who created the ear, hears us!
The Beloved who formed the eye, sees us!
Like the nations, we are accountable
            for our actions.
Where does knowledge come from, but
            the Heart of our heart.
        The Beloved knows our thoughts, and
            is the very Breath of our breath.

Blessed are those who have confessed their
            erring ways,
    who have asked for forgiveness.
Blessed are those whose burdens have
            been lifted,
    who are able to respond with love.
For the Beloved walks with them and
        speaks to them in the Silence;
With mercy and compassion, they
            are held in Love's heart;
        all who are at one with Love will
            live in peace and harmony.

Who will stand with Love and act
            with justice?
        Who will speak out to silence
            the oppressors?

Had the Beloved not come to my rescue,
my soul would still dwell in
the land of darkness.
When I recognized my wrongdoings.
your steadfast Love renewed me,
O Compassionate One.
When the cares of my heart were many,
your consolations comforted my soul.
Those who live separated from Love,
do not know the peace and joy of
walking with You.
They gather together to try those
who walk in peace,
and with worldly power, they
condemn the innocent.
Yet the Beloved is a stronghold,
the Comforter, the refuge
of my soul.
The statutes of Truth are certain;
and the Awakening, a promise
to be fulfilled;
Who will be ready for the
new dawn?

Psalm 95

O come, let us sing to the Most High
Creator of the Cosmos;
let us make a joyful song to
the Beloved!

Let us come to the Radiant One with
thanksgiving,
with gratitude let us offer our
psalms of praise!
For the Beloved is Infinite, the
Breathing Life of all.
The depths of the earth belong to Love;
the height of the mountains,
as well.
The sea and all that is in it,
the dry land and air above
were created by Love.
O come, let us bow down and give
thanks,
let us be humble before the
Blessed One!

For the Beloved is Supreme, and
we, blessed to be invited to
friendship
as companions along the Way!

O that today we would harken to the
Beloved's voice!
Harden not your hearts, as in
days of old,
that you be not separated from Love.
Be not like those who hear the Spirit's Voice
and heed it not,
thinking to be above the Teacher.
For life is but a breath in the
Eternal Dance,
a gift to be reverenced with trust,
an opportunity to grow in spirit
and truth,

That in passing into new Life, you enter
into the new Jerusalem.

Psalm 96

O sing to the Cosmos a new song;
sing to the Beloved, all the earth!
Sing to the Creator, and bless the Name
above all names;
sing praises to the Glorious One
from day to day.
Declare the splendor of the Radiant One
to all nations,
the marvelous works of Love
to all peoples!
For great is the Beloved, and greatly
to be praised;
reverence Love above all else.
For where your thoughts are,
reveals that which you treasure;
seek only the true Treasure.
Truth and integrity live with Love;
strength and beauty dwell
with the Beloved.

Yield to Love, O families of the earth,
yield to Love's glory and strength!
Yield to Love and learn of justice;
make of yourselves an offering
and be guided by Love!

Bow down in adoration and holiness;
for worthy is the Beloved to be
praised in all the earth!

The Creator of the Cosmos reigns!
Yes, the world has been created,
gift to all generations;
let truth and justice give birth
to peace and harmony!
Let the heavens be glad, and let
the earth rejoice;
let the seas laugh, and all
that fills them;
let the fields exult, and
everything in them!
Then shall the trees of the forest
sing for joy
before the coming of the Beloved,
who reigns in glory!
For through Love will come truth
and justice,
offering all the people gifts
of new Life.

Psalm 97

The Bestower of Life reigns with mercy,
let the earth rejoice!
Let the heavens be glad!

Justice preserves creation, allowing it
         to blossom and thrive;
      hidden within creation, You are
         the Heart of everything.
Fire goes before You, burning away the
         chaff and the tares.
Your Light enlightens the world;
         there is none to compare with You,
         O Great Transformer!
All of creation is clothed with
         your majesty, mirroring
      your Love throughout the cosmos.

The heavens proclaim your righteousness;
         and the peoples behold your glory.
Those who walk in darkness dwell in a
         house of fear,
      zealously following their desire
         for power;
      they live in the shadows of reality.
Heaven delights and rejoices when
         a hardened heart breaks open and
         recognizes Love's ever-patient
         Presence abiding within.
For You, O Beloved, encompass and bless
         all the earth;
      You forgive our wrongdoings and
         welcome us home.

You, O Beloved, are known by those who
         are true to the Promise,
      You are the Light of the saints;
      You hide yourself in every soul.
Light dawns for the just, and joy for
         the upright of heart.

Rejoice in the Most High, O people of
        the Light,
    and give thanks to the Radiant One,
        the Bestower of Life!

∾

Psalm 98

O sing to the Beloved a new song,
        for Love has done marvelous
            things!
By the strength of your Indwelling
        Presence,
    we, too, are called to do
        great things;
    we are set free through Love's
        forgiveness and truth.
Yes, your steadfast Love and faithfulness
    are ever-present gifts
        in our lives.
All the ends of the earth have seen
    the glory of Love's Eternal Flame.

Make a joyful noise to the Beloved
        all the earth;
    break forth into grateful song
        and sing praises!
Yes, sing songs of praise extolling
        Love's way;
    lift up your hearts with
        gratitude and joy!

Let the voices of all people blend
in harmony,
in unison let the people
magnify the Beloved!

Let the sea laugh, and all that
fills it;
the world and those who
dwell in it!

Let the waters clap their hands;
let the hills ring out with joy
Before the Beloved, who radiates Love
to all the earth.
For Love reigns over the world
with truth and justice
bringing order and balance to
all of Creation.

Psalm 99

Awaken, O you people! Entrust your
hearts to Love.
For the Beloved reigns supreme;
let all the earth give thanks!
Your unseen Presence is great in
the land;
You sit with the leaders of nations.

Let them be silent and guided by
                your Voice!
                Holy are You!
You are mighty and love justice,
        You establish equity;
Out of the Silence, your Word can
                be heard in the land
            inviting the nations to live
                in peace.
Listen O you people! Open your hearts
            to the Beloved,
        that Truth may be born anew!

Many who have gone before you followed
                the Beloved's Voice.
            the unknown saints of all
                generations.
        They surrendered themselves into
            the Beloved's hands,
        and walked with confidence.
They were guided through difficult times,
                keeping to Love's way,
            and trusting in Love's promises.

O Heart of all hearts, You answered
                their prayers;
            With mercy, You forgave them their
                wrongdoings, always
        inviting them to new life.
Sing praises to the Beloved, and
        aspire to ascend the holy
            mountain.
        Holy are You, O Giver of Life!

Psalm 100

Sing a joyful noise to the Beloved
all peoples of the earth!
Serve Love with a glad heart!
Join hands in the great
Dance of Life!

Know that the Beloved of your heart
is the Divine Presence!
Love created us, and we belong to
the Most High;
We are born to be loving,
expressions of the Creator's
Divine Plan.

Open the gates of your heart
with gratitude
and enter Love's court
with praise!
Give thanks to the Beloved,
bless Love's holy Name!

For Love is of God, and lives
in your heart forever,
With faith, truth, and joy, now
and in all that is to come.
Alleluia! Amen!

Psalm 101

I sing of loyalty and of justice;
    to You, O Beloved, I sing.
I give heed to the Way that
      leads to peace.
    Making a home in our hearts,
You are our loving Companion and Friend.

May I walk with integrity
      where'er I go,
May I see You in all creation!

May I be a mirror of your Love
    to all that I meet;
May I reflect the freedom of your
      Truth, and live
    as a beneficial presence in
      the world.

Forgive me, O Merciful One, if I turn
      from those in need.
Humble me if I become arrogant
      and greedy.
    Embrace me with your Presence.

I accompany those who love You,
    that I may grow in
      wisdom;
I enter into the Silence, into the
      Eternal Light,
    and listen for your gentle Voice.
For, no one who oppresses another,
    who keeps company with injustice,
    will dwell in the house of Love.

And, no one who prefers darkness
　　　will live in the glory of Light.

In the morning I offer myself to You
　　　　　in prayer,
　　　by night I surrender to You
　　　　　in trust;
O, that I might walk in the Light
　　　　　with a grateful heart,
　　　and radiate peace to the world!

Psalm 102

Hear my prayer, O Merciful One;
　　　let my cry come to You!
I long to see your face in
　　　　　the day of my distress!
Incline your ear to me;
　　　be quick to answer in the
　　　　　day when I call!

For the days pass away like smoke,
　　　a fire within consumes me.
My heart is broken, the fragments
　　　　　scattered to the winds.
　　　I have lost my appetite.
My groanings never cease; day and
　　　　　night I call to You.

I lay and wait, expecting vultures
        to devour me,
        dry and barren as the desert
                sands.
I lie awake, like a lone bird on
        the rooftop.
All the day my fears well up,
        threatening to overwhelm me.
Bread turns to ashes in my mouth,
        and tears mingle with my drink.
Because I feel so far from You, fear
        separates me from your Presence,
My days are like an evening shadow;
        I wither away like grass.

Yet You, O Comforter, are ever near,
        your kindness is made known to
                all generations;
You answer the prayers of those
        who cry to You.
Come! Melt every heart;
        the appointed time is nigh.
Those who trust in You find solace
                for their souls;
        tears soon turn to joy.
All who reverence and honor the
                Beloved,
        are nourished and held by Love.
For You, O Healer, invite us to
                wholeness, to be
        co-creators along Love's way.
You hear the cries of the afflicted,
        and answer their prayer.
Yet beware! Our thoughts are also
                our prayers,
May they be for the well-being of all!

Let this be recorded for generations
          to come,
     so that a people yet unborn may
          praise the Beloved:
That You come down from the
          Holy Mountain,
     to live in every receptive heart.
You hear the groans of the prisoners,
     liberating those doomed to die.
Let all nations declare the glory
          of your Holy Name
And gather together in peace to honor
          the Creator of All.

Though my strength be broken
          in mid-course,
     and my days shortened,
I cry to You, "Would that this cup
          be taken from me,
     You who are everlasting;
Yet, into your Hands will I commend
          my soul."

Of old You laid the foundation
          of the earth
     and the heavens to reflect
          your glory.
Even should they perish, your Love
          will endure,
     and You will raise us up
          to new Life.

Our lives are like the seasons,
          and they pass away;
     yet You remain constant and sure,
          your years have no end.

All generations to come will call
upon You, until all
peoples return to your Heart
in the Realm of Love.

Psalm 103

Bless the Beloved, O my soul,
and all that is within me;
I bless your Holy Name!
Bless the Beloved, O my soul,
and remember the goodness
of Love.
You forgive our stubborness
You heal our disease,
You save us from the snares
of fear,
You crown us with steadfast
Love and Mercy,
You satisfy our every need and
renew our spirit like
the eagle's.

Through You comes peace and
justice for all who are
oppressed.
You make known the pathway of
truth,
and guide us on the Way.

You are merciful and gracious,
    quelling our anger with your
       patient Love.
You love us more than we can ask
       or imagine;
    in truth, we belong to You.
For You understand us,
    requiting us not according to our
       ignorance and error.
As far as the heavens are high above
       the earth,
    so great is your loving response
       toward those who are humble;
So far does your enduring strength
    uphold those who face the
       darkness within.
As parents are concerned for their
       children,
    so You come to those
       who reach out in faith.
For our ways are known, our weaknesses
    seen with compassion.

As for humanity, our days are like
       the grass;
    we flourish like a flower of
       the field;
When the wind passes over,
       it is gone,
    and that place knows it no more.
Yet the steadfast Love of the Beloved
    is from everlasting to everlasting
       to those who Awaken,
    and justice to all generations,

To those who remember your Promises,
and follow your Voice.

The Beloved's home is in our hearts,
as we discover in the Silence.
Bless the Beloved, O you angels,
you faith-filled ones who hear
the Word,
following the Voice of Love!
Bless the Beloved, all you people,
those who abandon themselves
into Love's hands!
Praise the Beloved, praise all of Creation!
Praise the Beloved, O my soul!

Psalm 104

Bless the Radiant One, O my soul!
O Heart of my heart, You are
so very great!
You are clothed with justice and
mercy,
arrayed in Light as your
fine attire.
You stretch over the heavens
like a tent,
your Radiance covering the
waters;

You shine through the clouds, and
　　　ride on the wings of the wind;
The wind, like the Breath of Life,
　　　　　carries your Voice,
　　　　Fire refines the dross of
　　　　　our souls.

You set the earth on its foundations,
　　　　　strong and secure.
You covered it with the deep
　　　　　like a garment, with
　　　　many waters that life might
　　　　　come forth.
At your Word, the waters divided,
　　　becoming rivers and lakes and
　　　　　mighty oceans;
　　　　storms came to ensure the balance
　　　　and to renew the earth.
The mountains rose, the valleys became
　　　　　　low
　　　in the places that You did appoint.
You brought harmony to all the earth,
　　　that life might spring forth
　　　　in abundance.

You created springs to flow into the
　　　　　valleys;
　　　they flow between the hills,
Giving drink to every creature of
　　　　　the field,
　　　quenching their thirst as your
　　　　　Living Water quenches ours.
With the air, You have given birds
　　　　their habitation;
　　　they sing among the branches.

· *204* ·

The majesty of Creation is seen
            throughout the land,
    the sounds of Creation mingle
            with the music of the spheres.

Through your Love, grass came forth
            for the cattle,
    and plants for us to cultivate,
That we might have food from the earth,
            and wine, the fruit of the vine,
Oil and healing herbs of many varieties,
            and bread, our daily sustenance.
The trees are watered abundantly and
            with the sun,
    provide the air we breathe.
Every living creature has its home:
    the birds nest in trees, the wild
            goats upon the mountaintop;
    even the rocks provide protection.
You created the moon to mark the
            tides and seasons,
    the sun, that rises and sets
            in beauty.
In the darkness, when night comes,
    the creatures of the forest
            roam the earth.
They eat their fill, each according
            to their need;
    You provide their food.
When the sun rises, they disappear
            from sight
    and lie down in their dens.
As your people go forth to their work,
    You are there to guide them.

O You, who know all hearts, how
        manifold are your works!
    In wisdom You have created
        them all;
    the earth is filled with your
        creatures.
We look to the seas, great and wide,
    which teem with life innumerable,
    helping to maintain the balance.
O, that we might receive your gifts,
    taking only what is needed
        with grateful hearts.

All of creation looks to You,
    to give them food in
        due season.
When we are in harmony with You,
        the earth provides;
    yes, a bountiful harvest to be
        shared with all.
When we misuse what You have created
        for us,
    we blame You for the famine and
        destruction that ensues,
    and feel alienated from You.
Even so, You continue to send forth
        your Spirit, and
    the earth, though not without turmoil,
        is renewed.

The glory of the Radiant One endures
        forever, for
    the works of Love are sure.
You are ever-present to us, even as
        the earth trembles,

even as the mountains spew forth
ashes and smoke!
I will abandon myself into your hands
as long as I live;
I will sing praise to You
while I have breath.
May my meditations be pleasing to You,
for I rejoice and am glad in You.
May all who feel separated from You
open their hearts to new Life!
Praise the Creator of the Universe!
Bless the Heart of my heart,
O my soul!
Amen.

Psalm 105

O give thanks to the Beloved, and
open your hearts to Love.
Awaken! Listen in silence for the
Voice of the Counselor.
Sing praises with a glad heart
and give witness to the truth
with your lives!
Glory in the radiance of the Beloved;
let the hearts of those who call
upon You rejoice!
Seek the One who is Life, your strength,
walk harmoniously in Love's Presence!

Remember that you are not alone, for
      through Love doubt and fear
         are released;
O people of the earth, ever bear
      in mind
        the unity of diversity in the
          Divine Plan!

You are the Promise of our
        wholeness,
      You await our readiness to
        choose Life.
Your covenant of Love stands firm
        through all ages;
      You forgive us when we stray
        far from Home.
Help us to learn to trust You,
      to untangle the webs of illusion
        that we have made.
As we sift through our dreams,
      guide us to the only Dream
        that brings peace—
knowing we belong to You.
Give us wisdom and courage to release
      all that binds us;
      for, to let go of what is built
        on illusion is to find new life.

O Divine Presence, as we surrender
      our hearts to You,
      teach us to be worthy of trust.
O, that what we think and speak
      might be in accord with our
        highest aspirations,

That our faces might shine with
        openness,
     reflecting integrity and honesty
        within,
That we would choose to live in peace
        and harmony,
     our decisions made in accordance
        with Love.
Upon the path of trust, O friends,
     we need not judge ourselves
        or others,
For, as we reverence all life,
     the beauty and unity of diversity
        will be seen.

Gentle us, O Compassionate One, that
     we tread the earth lightly
        and with grace,
Spreading peace, goodness, and love,
     without harm to any creature.
For in gentle serenity is strength
        and assurance;
     confusion and suspicion find
        no home here.
In all things may we be grateful,
     our hearts open to joy.
O Mighty Counselor, speak to us
        within our hearts;
     let your Voice be heard.
And as we listen and heed your Way,
     joy will be our song of thanks.
As You lead us into the Silence,
     we become friends with solitude.

With trust in You our lives become
              simple,
          assurance and peace, leaving
              no room for fear.
All that we have is gift from you,
              O Gracious Beloved,
          all that we are is Yours
              as well.
May we come to see that all
              we give to others,
          we give to ourselves and You.

As the earth produces abundant
              harvests,
          when the sun and rain nourish
              the seeds,
So our fruits bless others as
          we grow in trust and love.
Teach us, O Merciful One, to have
              generous hearts,
          offering all we are in the
              name of Love.
As spring and summer follow
              the autumn and winter,
          so our lives have their seasons.
Help us to live in the eternal
              moment,
          awaiting your perfect timing
              in all things.
May we be content to wait in peace,
          until You stir the waters within
              to act;
          may we be patient with ourselves
              and with others.

O that we may have the light of wisdom,
      the steadfastness of faith!
In You alone is our trust, O Holy One,
      walking your Way is
            the truth that sets us free.
O that we may open our minds and
            hearts, and
      welcome You into our home,
That we may live each day
            conversing with You,
      O Loving Companion Presence!

As You have led all generations
      through times of turmoil and war,
Guide us now, O Blessed One,
      along the paths of peace.
May the people of all nations
      break the bonds of fear-filled
            oppression;
      may they bless one another
            with forgiveness.
      Blessed be the One who lives
            and dwells among us!

Psalm 106

Giver of Life, we praise You!
      Bestower of all gifts, we give
            You thanks, for
      your steadfast Love endures
            forever!

Who can tell of your generosity in
            all generations,
        the rich variety of the living
            cosmos?
Blessed are they who recognize the
        Gift, and
        who follow the precepts of your
            Life at all times.

You remember us, O Beloved, as we
            journey through life;
        help us to live the Mystery,
That we may fulfill our divine destiny,
        that we may co-create with You,
        that we may live into our
            divine birthright.
Stand by us that we may become poor
        in spirit,
        acknowledging our own weaknesses
            that lead us astray.
Teach us to be patient with ourselves,
        that we might offer the gift
            of patience to others;
O, that we might learn to be calm,
        to persevere with utter trust
        as we face the fears that
            bind us.
We yearn for all that will bring us
            new life,
        we long for your very Presence
            among us;
Comfort us, O Beloved, with the
            tranquility of your Spirit;
        lead us into calm waters.

Yes, the Comforter will nourish
            our souls, and
        gentle us, that we may be pliant
            in Love's hands.
The earth itself will reap the
            blessing of those
        who become beneficent and live
            with integrity.
We listen for your Voice, O Giver
            of the Journey, and
        we praise You with grateful hearts!

Breathing Life of all, we hunger for You;
        and we thirst for purity of heart.
Awaken us to all that is holy,
            to the sacred,
        that our lives may be a reflection
            of You;
For we love You, and in our hearts
        we will to do your Will.

Breath of the Merciful, teach us the way
            of compassion,
        that we may heed the cries
            of the poor;
That we may be merciful to those
        who live in the bonds of prison,
            illness, and loneliness;
And, may we be strong voices in support
            of justice;
        may we offer forgiveness as
            a healing balm.

Your Teaching is joy to our hearts,
        O, Creator of the Dance.

May we become bearers of joy,
    we who are invited to share in
        the Cosmic Dance!
We pray for the gift of wisdom,
    that the motivations of our heart
        might be made pure,
That we may recognize the perfect
        timing of all things
    and know the seasons of
        the heart.
May we walk with faith all the days
        of our life—
    confident in your Living Presence,
        even in times of trouble,
    and with assurance for what is
        and all that is to be;
May we have faith in the unfolding of
        our lives, and
    radical trust in the universe!
Awaken us to the Oneness of all things,
    to the beauty and truth of Unity.
May we become aware of the interdependence
        of all living things, and
    come to know You in every thing,
        and all things in You.
For as we attune to your Presence
        within us,
    we know not separation, and
    joy becomes our dwelling place.

Quiet us, O Silent Speaker, that
        out of still spaces
    we may hear your Voice;
And, as we ponder the immensity of
        your gift to us of life,
    awe and wonder fill our hearts; for

From galaxies and the furthest stars
to the smallest atom in our heart,
You are the Flame of Love.
Forgive us, O Holy One, for our
wanton ways that have laid waste
to our planet!

May we embrace Creation as a whole,
and become attuned to all the world;
May we be blessing to the universe, and
see divinity in the within and
the without of all things.
O Great Hunter, search our beings,
awaken our inner eyes and ears;
Come into the Secret Room of our hearts
and be our Guest.
Help us to understand and embrace the
fears that bind us,
That we may grow in courage, and
challenge injustice where'er it
prevails.
For as we withdraw our projections
upon others,
balance and harmony adorn us;
Our peaceful presence becomes blessing
to the world;
we become at one with all of
Creation.
Yes, as our hearts are awakened to
your Presence within us,
we are led back to the Source
of all life.

Call us, O Beloved, to spaces of
solitude, and
times to befriend the Silence;

That we may ever know, O Divine One,
    that You are with us always,
      we cannot hide from your Love.
For You, in whom we live and have
          our being,
    distinguish not our race or creed;
Male and female are equal in your sight,
    You take pleasure in the richness
      of diversity!
May we learn the bitter lesson of
      judgment—
    'tis but a mirror of ourselves
      we see.
Increase our willingness to risk, Beloved,
    to be open to change and surprises
      by the Spirit,
    to be willing to suffer that our
      souls may grow;
For our souls increase as we let go,
    as we release all that diverts
      and separates us from You.

Gather us together, O Healing Presence,
    forgive us for the destruction we
      wrought among the nations,
That we may live in peace with all
      people
    and bring glory to your Name.

Blessed are You, Creator of All that is,
    we praise You from everlasting to
      everlasting!
With joy and gratitude, let all the
      people say, "Amen!"
Praises be to You, our Joy!

Psalm 107

We give thanks to You,
    who are the Source of Love;
    whose Light shines forth
        throughout the universe!
Come, awaken our hearts that
    we might do your Work;
For, without You, we can do nothing;
    'tis your Love that loves
        through us.

Gather us in from all the lands,
    from the east and the west,
    from the south and the north.
Let all who are hungry and thirsty,
    whose souls are faint within
        them,
Cry out to the Most Merciful to give
        them succor,
    to nourish them with healing
        love;
For fear cannot live where love, grace,
        and gentleness abide.
Enter into the Great Silence,
    where you may hear the voice
        of the Beloved,
Who satisfies the hungry soul,
    and quenches the thirsty with
        streams of Living Water.

Yes, attune yourselves to the small
        still Voice within,
    stay true to your heart's Center.

For through your inner being Truth
          and Wisdom are heard;
      the resource to break all bonds
          is found there, too.
Has no one ever told you that
      truth is written on the scrolls
          of your heart,
      that the Beloved dwells therein?
O peoples of the Light, Awaken to
      the knowledge that lives
          within you!
Come out of the darkness and gloom;
      break through the fears that
          hold you prisoner.
Do you not know your destiny is
      to be a light unto the world,
      a bearer of peace and harmony?
O let your light shine as a very ray
      of the Radiant One's own Light!

And know yourself! Let your aim be
      to recognize who you are.
Aspire to live as sons and daughters
          of Divine Love,
      to enshrine the earth with
          divinity,
To honor all relationships as sacred, and
      to live in peace and in balance with
          all living things.
Acknowledge the sacredness of
          every path,
      albeit different from your own;
In this way you honor the Great Mystery
      and the wonder of all life!

Remember always to offer grateful hearts
in thanksgiving to the One
who lives among us!

O, that you might learn to see
with your heart,
to hear and think with your
heart, as well!
Many there are who boast of their
own deeds,
who are proud of their power
over others.
Where will they be when storms arise,
when earthquakes shatter the
rocks of their hearts?
Only the humble will call to the
Spirit
to help them in times of distress;
The wise wait not for trouble,
but communicate with the Counselor
in all things.
Enter the Holy Temple of your heart,
and learn to still the tumult
of the mind;
For, to be serence even in the midst
of chaos,
is to know the efficacy of
calmness.
Peace dwells in the heart of silence,
compassion and mercy abide
there, as well.
Come, let us give thanks to the
Heart of all hearts,
giving praise for the unlimited
gifts of Love!

Let us pray for the well-being of all life,
    and learn to dance in harmony
        with the cosmos!

Who will offer the dance of their
        own life,
    as a creation of devotion
        and beauty?
Only those who have come through
        the darkness
    and walk now in the Light
Can offer their lives in Service
        to build the new world,
    where justice and freedom
        will truly flourish.
Awaken, all you who are yet asleep,
    let us plant seeds for the
        commingling of heaven
        and earth;
For the Energy of Love radiates in
        everything, and
    receptive hearts are purified
        by its Fire.
Blessed are the children of Light,
    for they know their home in
        the Universal Heart.

Let your heart be clear and simple,
    and your soul filled with Light;
Enter the place of gentleness,
    the heart-space of the Beloved,
        the embodiment of Love!
For we are invited to radiate the
        Divine Presence,
    to be blessing to one another;

Thus do we become the very image
that we reflect.
Whoever is wise, let them ponder
these things,
let all people reflect on the
gifts of the Beloved.

Psalm 108

My heart is united with
Your Heart, O Beloved!
I sing, and I will sing praises!
My soul is awakened:
O joy, O gratitude!
I arise to the new dawn!
I give thanks to You, Beloved,
among the peoples,
I sing praises to You among
the nations.
For your steadfast Love is great
through all the world,
your faithfulness remains
for all eternity.
Be exalted, O Radiant One, throughout
the universe!
Let your Glory extend to the
ends of the earth!
That your friends may be set free
from fear,
Come to our aid, waken us all!

For You have been our Promise for
          all generations:
     "Come to Me when your hearts
          are heavy,
     and I will give you rest.
For as I am in you, so do you
          live in Me;
     we are One in the Spirit of Love.
Be my messengers of peace;
     be bearers of mercy and justice;
     let Love triumph over fear."

Who will answer the invitation of Love?
     Who will lead others into
          the new dawn?
Stay Awake, O my soul, to
          the Beloved within;
     O, that I might shine as a light
          in the world!
Released from the darkness within,
     I extend your Peace
               out to the world;
     for You are my Peace and
          my Light!
With You I can do all things;
     into your Heart I commend
          my soul always.

Psalm 109

Be not silent, O You whom
               I praise!
Many are the fears that envelop me,
          causing me to act without
                    integrity.
I become boastful that others may
                    not see me tremble,
          and I speak ill even of my
                    friends.
In return, I become alienated from
                    those who love me, and
          from You to whom I pray.
Hear my plea, O Compassionate One,
          in your mercy, come to my aid.

You appoint an angel to watch
                    over me,
          to protect me as I face
                    my fears.
As I meet temptation, You strengthen me;
          my faith and courage increase.
May the day dawn, when I become
                    like the eagle,
          and soar to lofty heights!
May I break the fetters of fear and
          welcome peace into my heart!
May I grow in wisdom and abandon
                    myself
          to You with radical trust, and
          though I may suffer, may I
                    reach maturity of soul!

May I open myself to change,
          to being guided by the Spirit;

may I risk the unknown and
live into the Mystery!
Awaken me to the holy, to the divinity
of all creation;
O, that I might honor the sacredness
of all life!
May all the resentment and bitterness
that live in me
be transformed by your Love!
Help me to recognize the unmet needs that
have turned to desire and lust;
create a clean heart within me!
Let all that has been stored in secret
come forth into the radiance
of your Light;
O, wash away my hidden faults!

For You are kind and merciful,
ever searching for ready hearts,
and comforting those who cry
out to You!
Implant your gifts within my spirit,
that I might offer them out
to those in need!
For, I long to do your Will, to
co-create in joy,
to become a beneficent presence
in the world!
Become like a garment wrapped
around me,
clothe me in the raiment
of your Love!

Then will I be strong to face
my fears

with a love that is firm and
sure.
For You, O Heart of all hearts,
are the Thread
that connects each one of us,
that defines the interconnectedness
of all being!
Though I am weak and yet have miles
to go,
your steadfast Love will lead
me Home.
Fear yields itself to Love and
cannot withstand the Light;
Just as one lit candle dispels
the darkness,
each ray of love eases the
pangs of fear.
O, Giver of the Journey, companion me
along the way;
then will I recognize your Face
in each one I meet.

Yes, guide me into wholeness, harmony,
and balance,
that I may be a peaceful
presence.
Let me give witness to your Way,
that others may grow in
trust and truth!
O, Great Awakener, open the eyes
and ears of my heart;
let my dormant talents be
made known.
For, with jubilation would I enter
your Presence, to
love and serve in the great Plan!

With loud voice I will extol You,
O Creator of the Cosmos;
I will praise You among the
peoples!
For You are Comfort and Blessing
to all who call;
You love us into new Life!

Psalm 110

The Beloved says to all who will
hear,
"Come, walk with Me. Let us
give birth to a new Earth!"

For, the Spirit is the One who makes
all things new, and ever
awaits our "yes" to the
Dance!
Those who offer themselves freely,
without reserve,
are guided through life's rough
paths.
Light beckons to light; divine dignity
adorns all in holy array.
The Promise holds true forever,
to all generations!
"As companions of the Most High,
come! Claim your home in the
Universal Heart!"

You, O Divine Breath, dwell within
               our hearts; with
           unconditional Love, You assuage
               our fears.
You call us to holiness, to justice,
               and integrity,
        to free those bound by oppression,
        to bring light where ignorance
              and darkness dwell.
Come! Drink from the streams of
               Living Water.
        Come! Feast on the Bread of Life.

Psalm 111

Praise the Beloved, O my soul!
I will give thanks to You with
               my whole heart,
        to all who will listen, I will
               tell of your goodness.
Wondrous is Creation, Great Builder;
        I take pleasure in pondering
               your Work.
Full of honor and integrity are
               your teachings;
        those who follow them will
               find new life.
You lift the hearts of those who
               suffer;
        You come to them in their need.

Your steadfast Love is food for
the soul,
nourishment in times of fear.
You are ever-mindful of your
covenant,
a very Presence to the weary
and afflicted.
Your Voice is truth to those with
ears to hear,
your precepts are sure;
Written on the hearts of your
people, they are
to be lived forever with
faith-filled love and assurance.
You bring new life to the world;
Yes! life in abundance is your
gift to us.
Holy and glorious is your Name!
Reverence for You, O Holy One, is the
beginning of wisdom;
a good understanding have all
who practice it.
Your Spirit endures for ever!

Psalm 112

Praises be to You, O Gracious One!
Blessed are those who reverence
    the Holy One, who delight in
        Love Consciousness!
For they dwell with the Beloved,
    and their children will learn
        of peace and justice.
Abundance and wholeness will be
        their heritage,
    and truth will be their banner.
Light penetrates the darkness for those
        who face their fears;
    Love stands by them with mercy
    and forgiveness.

It goes well for those who are loving
        and kind,
    who live their days with justice
    and integrity.
They become co-creators with the
        Divine One;
    they bless the world with their
    presence.
In times of trouble, they know not fear;
    their hearts are firm, trusting in
    your Loving Companion Presence.
Yes, their hearts are steady, they
        are not afraid,
    even their enemies are blessed
    by their love.
They are generous and give freely;
    the needy are offered shelter
    and food;

justice and mercy make their
home there; and
their righteousness endures
forever.
The unloving are witness to this;
who knows when the Seed will
find a fertile heart?
The fruits of those who know Love
are blessing to all!

Psalm 113

Sing praises to the Beloved
of all hearts!
Sing praises, all you who would
honor Love,
sing praises to the Architect
of the universe!

Bless the Holy One from this time
forth
and forever more!
Aspire to know the Unknowable,
to enter fully into the
Great Mystery,
to be fertile ground to the
Heart-seed of Love.
Aspire to gifts of the Spirit,
be open to Grace and express
gratitude!

Who is like the Blessed One,
        the One who is Infinite Love,
                Power, and Wisdom,
Who enters into human hearts
        and brings comfort to those
                in need?
Yes, those who call upon the
                Merciful One,
        are lifted up and blessed with
                new life;
They wear a crown of joy,
        as they recognize their
                Oneness with Spirit.
Come, all who suffer and are
                heavy-laden,
        open your hearts to Love!
Sing praises to the Heart of all hearts!

Psalm 114

Come, all you who have wandered
                far from the path,
        who have separated yourselves
                from Love;
A banquet is prepared for you in the
                heart's Secret Room.

There you will find the way Home;
        a welcome ever awaits you!

Even as you acknowledge the times
you have erred,
the forgiveness of the Beloved
will envelop you.

Call upon the Beloved when fear
arises,
when you feel overwhelmed;
The Eternal Listener will heed
your cry;
you will find strength to face
the shadows.

Befriend all that is within you,
discover the Sacred Altar within
your heart.
Then will abundant blessings enter
your home; and, you
will welcome the Divine Guest
who is ever with you.
You are never alone!

Psalm 115

Those who teach illusion are
ignorant
as are those who trust in them.

O, people of the earth, trust in the
Blessed One,
in the Holy One, who is your
very life!

O, nations of the world, put your
            trust in the Blessed One,
      in the Holy One, who is your
            Guide and Counselor!
You, who open your hearts to Love,
            will find inner peace,
      through the Holy One, who is
            your Teacher!

The Beloved is ever mindful of us,
            and blesses us.
      Love will bless the peoples;
      Love will bless the nations;
The Beloved will bless those who
            invite Love within,
      who open wide the door, and
      who bless the world with
            their presence.

May you call upon the Holy One,
            you and your children!
May you be guided by the Spirit of Truth,
      who dwells within your heart!
The heavens declare the glory of
            the Creator,
      the earth, too, is filled
            with wonder, gifts
            of Love.
Fear not for your life; for death
      is but a doorway to new birth;
      the Beloved has shown us
            the way to Eternal Life.
Let us trust the Holy One from this
            time forth and forevermore.
Sing praises to the Living Presence, to
            You, Life of all life!

Psalm 116

Receive my love, O Beloved, You who
        hear my voice and my supplication.
You incline your ear to me, and
      I call upon You with trust
        both day and night.
When the snares of fear encompass me,
      when the pangs of loneliness
        envelop me,
      I suffer distress and anguish.
Then I call upon You, my Rock:
      You come to my aid,
      Your strength upholds me.

Gracious are You, just and true;
      Heart of all hearts, You are
        merciful and forgiving.
You preserve the simple; when
      I am humbled, You lift
        me up.
Return, O my soul, to your rest;
      for You, O Loving Friend,
        bestow grace upon grace,
        a balm for my soul.

You raise me up to new life;
      You dry my tears, and
        guide my feet on straight paths.
Now, I walk hand in hand with Love
      in the land of the Awakened ones.
I keep my faith, even in times
        of great turmoil;
I invite others to Awaken to the joy
      of your Presence.

What shall I render to You for all
　　　　your goodness to me?
I will drink the chalice of Love
　　　and praise You, who have done
　　　　wondrous things;
I will bear witness to You,
　　　　　O Bread of Life,
　　　in the presence of all the people.
Precious to You are all whose
　　　　will decreases,
　　　who abandon themselves into
　　　　your Will.
O Beloved, consider me your friend;
　　　I long to co-create with You.
　　　For You have loosed the bonds
　　　　of fear in me.
I will offer to You the gift
　　　　of gratitude
　　　and acknowledge your Loving
　　　　Presence with joy.
I will bear witness to You,
　　　　　O Giver of Life,
　　　in the presence of all the people,
In the Sacred Altar of my heart,
　　　in your midst, O Beloved.
Praises be to You! For You dwell
　　　　within the heart of everything!

Psalm 117

*P*raise the Most Merciful, all nations!
　　Extol the Holy One, all peoples!
For great is the Blessed One's Love
　　　　towards us;
　　　The Beloved's faithfulness
　　　　endures forever.
Praises be to the Heart of all hearts!

Psalm 118

*W*e give thanks to You,
　　　　O Beloved,
　　　for You are kind;
　　　your steadfast Love endures
　　　　forever!

Let every nation proclaim,
　　　"Your steadfast Love endures
　　　　forever."
Let all the people cry,
　　　"Your steadfast Love endures
　　　　forever."
Let those who reverence You sing,
　　　"Your steadfast Love endures
　　　　forever."

Out of my distress I called upon You;
　　　You answered, setting me
　　　　on a new path.

With You beside me, I do not fear.
What can others do to me?
You live within me and answer
my prayer as
I face the fears that
well up from within.
It is better to abandon yourself
to the Beloved
than to trust in yourself alone.
It is better to surrender to Love's will
than to seek the riches
of the world.

When all my fears surrounded me,
I acknowledged your Presence
within me!
When they surrounded me on every side,
I gave thanks for your Companioning
Presence!
They surrounded me like bees, and
they threatened to overwhelm me;
in your strong Presence,
I faced them!
Though they arose like an army,
You stood firm beside me.
You are my strength and my song;
You are my Counselor and my Friend.

Harken to songs of victory,
to the music of my soul:
"You, O Loving Presence, have been
my strength,
You have stood beside me
in the darkness,

You have walked with me
into the light!"
I shall not give in to fear,
but I shall live in peace
and give witness to your
saving grace.
You turned your face from my
weaknesses, and
You opened the door leading
to new life.

Yes, You opened to me the gates
of truth and justice
that I might enter through them.
Praise be to You, O Merciful One!

This is the Door to Life;
those who know Love shall
enter through It.

I give thanks to You, O Beloved, who
answer our prayers
and invite us to new Life.
The stone which the builders rejected
has become the foundation
of our lives.
This, O Eternal Listener, is your Work;
it is marvelous in our eyes.
This is the day which You have made;
let us rejoice and be glad in it!

Remain ever by our side, O Friend!
We welcome You into our hearts
as Loving Companion Presence!

Blessed are all who enter through
   your gates!
  Blessed are all who dwell in
   the house of Love!
For You lead the Way, You forgive
   our misguided ways, and
  You bring Light into darkness.
Come, all you who will, partake of
   the Great Banquet!

You are my Beloved, and I will
   give thanks to You;
  You are my Beloved, greatly
   will I praise You!

We give thanks to You, O Blessed One,
  for You are kind; your steadfast
   Love endures for ever!

Psalm 119

Blessed are those whose ways are
   blameless,
  who live with spiritual integrity!
Blessed are those who honor the
   Inner Being,
  who follow You with their
   whole heart,

Who enfold the world with love
     and walk on peaceful paths!
You have shown us the way of Truth,
     the way that leads to freedom.
O, that I might ever reflect the
          Light!
Then I shall know inner peace, as
     I surrender myself into
          your Hands.
I will praise You with a grateful
          heart,
     as I lean on your great
          kindness.
As I forsake the path of darkness,
     O have mercy on me!

How can the young keep to the
          straight path? Only
     by learning to listen to the
          still Voice within.
With all my heart I seek You;
     let me not wander from
          your teachings!
Your Love is imprinted upon my heart,
     that I may walk in your Light.
Blessed are You, O Counselor;
     guide me in all that I do,
That with my lips I may bear
     witness to the truth of your Way.
With your Word in my heart,
     I delight more than with the
          world's riches.
I listen in the Silence,
     awaiting the clarity of your
          counsel.

May I become a living fountain of joy
        as I give thanks for your
                bountiful blessings!

I offer myself into your Hands,
        that I may live fully
                into your Life.
Open my heart's eyes, that I may see
        the wondrous blessings of
                Creation.
I am a sojourner on earth; yet
        I know myself as a
                spiritual Being!
My soul is consumed with an intense
                longing to be
        blessed and sustained by You,
                O Divine Lover!
May I not be a bearer of disharmony,
        one who is arrogant and greedy;
Teach me to stand firm when faced with
                injustice and oppression,
        to be fervent in my stance
                for truth!
Even though fears rise up, may my eyes
        remain focused on You.
For in Love Consciousness do I delight;
        O my Counselor and Friend!

With my heart's ear I hear the
                injunction
        to pray for my enemies,
        even those who persecute me!
How can I, weak and fear-filled,
        heed this difficult teaching?

Help me to understand the way of
         your precepts, and
    the strength to follow through.
My soul is willing, O Merciful One,
    yet the body would flee.
Who is the enemy from whom I run,
      but the ego-fears hidden in the
        shadows within!
Strengthen me according to your Life,
    lead me gently into the Light.
For, I have chosen the way of
        faithfulness;
      with trust in You, I will face
      my own darkness.
I will not run from the illusions which
      beset me, so that
      each one may be transformed in
      and through your Love.

Help me to know, O Teacher,
      the path to follow;
    lead the way and I will come.
In your love is the power to calm
      the storms of adversity;
    show me the power of your
      forgiving Love.
O that I might learn to bless others
      selflessly,
    to be a silent benediction!
Incline my heart to Love Consciousness,
    and not to gain!
Turn my eyes from the world's
      temptations, and
      birth me into new Life.

Let me enter into the realm where
the aspirations of my soul may
become manifest.
Clothe me with compassion that
I may answer the cries of those
in need.
Do You see how I long to serve,
To co-create with You?
In your mercy, hear my prayer!

You ever enfold us in the power of
your boundless love,
according to your Promise to us;
You have implanted the Divine Seed
in every heart,
a Treasure beyond words.
Teach us to nurture that Seed so
it might blossom into fulness
and maturity.
O, Giver of Life, may we recognize
the Divine Seed in every person;
May we be sensitive to all we meet
along the way,
blessing and encouraging one
another;
May we know that who we are is
a reflection of You, the
Divine Seed we bear.
You are the Sunlight of our heart,
the Water that brings
forth Life!
Praises be to You, O Holy One
of Ineffable Power!

I meditate on the words that I hear as
        You whisper in my heart, words
                that refresh and renew my soul.
This is my comfort when doubts arise,
        the secret Promise of Life.
Though others do not understand me,
        assurance and peace in You
                sustain me.
Let my self-made spirit decrease,
        that I may be rich in your
                Divine Spirit!
Let me carry the crosses that
        come to me, with
        your strength to bear me up.
May I become hollow like the reed,
        so You may play your melody
                through me.
For I long to be attuned to the great
                song of the Cosmos,
        to know the song of inner praise!
O, that I might hear the Divine Melody
                within
        and give birth to a dancing star!
You are my portion;
        You are the sacred Gift of Life.
Though You speak to the ears of
                every heart, yet
        not every heart will hear You.
O friends, close not the eyes of
                your heart
                to the light of Truth!
Rejoice in the glorious and sacred
                Giver of Life,
        clothe yourself with joy!

Feel your heart expand in gratitude,
and learn from the earth
of humility.
I will sing praises to You throughout
the day, and
meditate on Love during
the night.
For You are Companion and Friend
to all who reverence your ways.
The earth is filled with Divine Love;
O, that I might know You in
all things!

You are fulfilling your covenant
within me,
O Faithful One, according to
your Promise.
Teach me good judgment and
understanding,
for I know your teachings
are sure.
Before, I was sorely afraid and
I went astray;
but now, I hold to your Word.
You are Love, and all Love comes
from You;
help me to share the
treasures of the heart.
May I come to live with patience,
waiting for your perfect timing
in all circumstances.
May tolerance make its home in me,
that I recognize You in
every heart.

May I be imbued with love and mercy
        making room for kindness in
            all situations.
For your ways are far richer
        than thousands of gold and
            silver pieces.

Your Hands and Love created and
            fashioned me;
        give me understanding that
            I may live fully in You.
Those who follow the ego are
            in darkness; may they
        see how You have transformed
            my life with light.
May they rejoice and turn away
            from empty paths;
        may they find hope in your Way.
May I always welcome love and
            assurance, and
        offer these gifts to those
        who weep and live in illusion.
Let your mercy and compassion wash
            over me,
        that I may ever work on behalf
            of justice.
And grant me a generous heart,
        O, my Friend and Teacher,
        for I would give freely of my time
            and energy in your Name.

Let my life give witness to You,
        to those filled with fear.
Create in me a clean heart,
        that your light might be seen!

_____

My soul sighs awaiting your
            living Presence; for
      I sense your Love and Light.
My heart wells up with gratitude
            and praise, as
      I recall the innumerable blessings
            You continually bestow.
When I ponder the plight of the world,
      my heart weeps for all the
            oppressed.
How long, O Merciful One, must we
            endure the greed,
      the arrogance of those who are
            in power—
Those whose hearts have turned
            from You,
      who follow not the way
            of Love,
Who have become blind to the Truth,
      and deaf to your Voice
            whispering in their hearts?

Awaken the people of earth, O You,
      who are the Great Awakener!
In your steadfast love, melt all hearts
      that have turned to stone;
            long have we awaited a great
            Spirit-quake.

O Holy One, Love Consciousness is
      firmly fixed in the heavens.
Your faithfulness endures to all
            generations;
      Love is the hope and promise
            of all the Earth.

Help us to reverence Her, to care
            for Her with compassion;
        for we have sorely misused Her.
If You had withheld your Love
            from us,
        we would have perished from
            our fears.
Your Truth is ever before us;
        by It, You have set us free.

I am yours, grace me with your Presence,
            for I would be a loving friend
                and companion to You.
I say to those I meet, "Come,
            the way is yours!
        Come, all you who are fearful
            and lonely!
Follow the sacred path of Truth;
        Come to the inner way of Light!"

O, how I love your friendship!
        I walk with You wherever I go.
Your Love is the life-giving force
            of Creation,
        imbue us with your living rays
            of peace and joy.
For, as we surrender ourselves to
            your living Presence,
        we will be filled with the
            radiance of Love.
As we open our hearts to the spiritual
            life,
        we will be filled with wisdom and
            freedom, ready to serve.

O, how glorious are the ways of the
        Spirit!
     How wondrous are your Works!
The path of love is sure, unhurried
       and filled with mystery.
How sweet are your words to my taste,
     sweeter than honey to my mouth!
Through your Mind I receive understanding;
     I no longer take pleasure in my
       former ways.

Yes, your Truth is a lamp to my feet
     and a light to my path.
You give me strength as I descend into
      the inner sanctum,
     to uncover the hidden blessings,
     to seek the treasures of the Spirit.
When I am filled with fear,
     I meditate upon your Light.
I yearn to have every doubt and fear
      quelled and transformed;
O, Heart of all hearts, bless me with
      your healing Light,
     that I may be a loving presence.

Though the ignorant lay snares for me,
     let me not stray from You.
Your Word is my heritage forever;
     yes, it is the joy of my heart.
I shall open my heart's ear to converse
      with You
     forever, to the end.

When I meditate upon your Light,
     my heart opens with compassion
      for all life.

This is how the veil is lifted,
      how the soul is filled with
        truth and light.
Then we will not judge others, and
      we will radiate love and healing
        to the world.
For as we develop the capacity to
      bless others,
      we will lighten the fears in
        the world.
Uphold us according to your Promise,
      that we may love;
      let not fear and illusions find
        a home in us.
Even should we go astray and wander
      far from You,
      You will ever love us.
We have only to return to You
      and acknowledge our regret; and
      You forgive us, refreshing our souls.
O friends, let us sing praises before
      such a Gift,
      before such all-enfolding Love,
        Wisdom, and Power!

O, that my soul would live from
      its innermost Being, and
      give witness to truth in thought,
        word, and deed!
For, only then will I see the glorious
      vision
      and hear the Voice of the Beloved.
Teach me the way of discernment
      that I make choices with integrity.

In your steadfast Love, may I know
the joy of responsibility for
all my deeds.
Give me courage for all the trials,
testings, and training as
I choose the spiritual life.

Breathe on me, O Breath of Inspiration,
in the silence of my tranquil heart,
infill me with your wisdom.
O, that I might radiate the compassion
and peace,
the truth and beauty of the Beloved!
Direct my steps, O Holy One, that
I may humbly walk with You.
The witness of your Life is
my model;
therefore my soul yearns for You.
The unfolding of your Way gives light;
it imparts understanding to
the simple.
My mouth pours forth praise continually,
for I am ever grateful for
your Promises.
You come to me and are gracious to me,
as You are to all who open
their heart's door.
Guide my steps according to your
Wisdom,
and show me how to lovingly
co-create with You.
Let me not be lured by the
world's values,
that I may walk the path of
wholeness.

May your face shine upon your
   friend, as
  You teach me of Love.
I weep over our wounded world,
   our earth ravaged by greedy,
    insensitive hands.

O friends, you who are fearful
   of Love,
  you, who live in loneliness,
Break open the locks of your
   heart's door,
   breathe deeply of sunlight's
    freedom and warmth.
Wander no longer in the storms of
   ignorance and fear; for
   the bonds of darkness will disappear
   as you enter the new dawn of Light!
Hold tightly to the hand of faith
   for strength through deep valleys;
Learn to trust in the One,
   who is ever your companion
   and guide.

Be not afraid of Love's touch,
   the Fire that consumes all
   dross;
For Love is the great transformer,
   burning away false ways of the
   past, and
   filling the heart with Light.
Awaken to the Indwelling Presence of
   the Beloved!
   Envision the beauty that Love
   brings forth!

When faced with slow progress, and
                seemingly endless delays,
        You enfold me in your patient
        Heart.
Let me recognize your perfect timing
                in all things,
        the fulness of your providence.
May I be so strong in your Spirit
        that all I do is inspired by You.
For You are loving, kind, and gentle;
        in You are all blessings.
Let me not be deaf to your Voice,
        nor suffer the pain of a
                rebellious soul.
Gentle me, O Loving Guide, that
                I may learn
        the wisdom of purity, patience,
                and peace.
Teach me of mercy, O You who are
                the Merciful One,
        that my soul may serve with You
                joyfully and with love.
O friends, open your heart to
                the divine life!
        Attune yourself to the Divine Guest
                within your Being!

For, when you come to know the
                Source of your life,
        love flows through you and
                radiates outward;
Harmony enters into your life,
        you see with new eyes.

All that once brought pain and
                suffering
        no longer affects the peace in
                your heart.
Through the healing forgiveness
        of Love,
        all past wrongs are righted;
Joy comes alive in your heart,
        the joy of understanding.
Then do you know the great
                Treasure,
        the pearl hidden in the Secret
                Realm within.
Glorious is the life of the soul
        when illumined by the
                Divine Spirit.
Search for it, friends, count not
        the years;
        enter into the stillness of
                your innermost being!

Abandon yourself to the Beloved,
        draw closer and closer to Love.
For when you dwell in peace within
        Love's heart,
        and know the Divine Spirit in
                your own heart,
You become as nothing, yet
        all things are yours.
As you radiate the healing love of
                your inmost Being
        into a suffering, scarred, yet
                ever-sacred world,
Offer grateful praise from the Chalice
        of your heart
        to the One who loves through you.

Great peace have those who co-create
with You,
who share the living wine of
your Spirit.
They know that all goodness comes
from your Divine Love,
the Source and Foundation of
all life.
Fill us, O Gracious One, with your
loving wisdom,
guide all hearts on paths
of peace.
When the journey seems long,
when we become discouraged
along the way,
You uphold and sustain us,
You restore us with your
blessed grace.
When we stumble and stray amid the
thorns on false paths,
we are ever humbled by your
forgiving Love.

You welcome us home as honored
guests,
back into the fold of your Heart.
You have prepared a garden for us,
a garden of joy hidden in
our hearts.
O friends, enter into this eternal
garden,
befriend the Guide who
awaits you.
Enter into the great, resounding Silence,
be still and know true peace;

Know the all-embracing life of Love;
and raise your voice with grateful
acclamations of praise!
Amen.

Psalm 120

In my distress I cry to You,
that You may come quickly
to comfort me:
"Be strong in me, that I might
face the darkness,
the despair that rises up
from the depths."

"I am bowed down with remorse:
for my inappropriate choices,
forgive me, O Healer.
For all my betrayals of others and
to my own soul,
forgive me, O Healer.
Bless my tears that flow like a
stream running to meet
the Living Waters of your Love.
Too long have I lived by my ego,
my desires blinding me
to your Love.
I yearn to live in peace; come quickly!
Strengthen me as I face
the illusions within!"

Psalm 121

My heart's eyes behold your
        Divine Glory!
    From whence does my help come?
My help comes from You,
    who created heaven and earth.

You strengthen and uphold me,
    You, who are ever by my side.
Behold! You who watch over the
        nations
    will see all hearts Awaken
        to the Light.

For You are the Great Counselor;
    You dwell within all hearts,
    that we might respond to the
        Universal Heart—
Like the sun, that nourishes us by day,
    like the stars that guide the
        wayfarer at night.
In You we shall not be afraid of
        the darkness, for
    You are the Light of our life.
May You keep us in our going out
        and our coming in
    from this time forth and
        forevermore.

Psalm 122

My spirit soared when a Voice
        spoke to me:
          "Come, come to the Heart
           of Love!"
How long I had stood within the
        house of fear
          yearning to enter the gates
           of Love!

The New Jerusalem, the Holy City,
        is bound firmly together;
All who seek the Heart of Love,
        those who have faced their fears,
Enter the gates in peace and with
        great joy,
          singing songs of thanksgiving.
There, in harmony with the cosmos,
        the community gathers united
          in love.

Pray for the peace of the world!
        May all nations prosper as one!
May peace reign among all peoples,
        and integrity dwell within
          every heart!
Then will friends and neighbors, and
        former enemies as well,
          cry out, "Peace be within you!"
For the good of the universe and
        in gratitude to the Beloved,
Let us serve the Holy One,
        of all nations
          with glad hearts.

Psalm 123

To You I lift up my spirit,
    You, who are enthroned
      in every heart!
For, as the young child holds tightly
    the hand of its parent,
As those in the throes of disease
    look to one who brings comfort,
So our spirits seek the Heart of Love,
    that we might find mercy
      and forgiveness.

Have mercy on us, O Compassionate One,
    have mercy,
    that we might turn from our
      blind and ignorant ways.
Too long our souls have been veiled
    by fear and illusion.
Have mercy, lead us to the
    path of wholeness, that
we may know the abiding Peace
    of the Beloved.

Psalm 124

If it were not for You, O Beloved,
    You who make all things new,
Fear and chaos would reign
    in every heart; in You
    will I trust forever.

When doubt threatens to overwhelm
and separate me,
when anger makes me blind,
Then You, O Merciful One, are
ever-ready
to Awaken the holy, the sacred
within me;
Then do your Living Streams of Grace
enfold me.

Blessed are You, who are a very
Presence to us,
a comfort to troubled hearts!
Grant us the strength of eagle wings,
the courage to soar to new heights!
Break within us the bonds of fear
that we may live with love!

Our guidance comes from You,
O Counselor,
Blessed are You, O Giver of Life!
Beloved of my heart!

Psalm 125

Those who put their trust in You
are like giant trees
standing firm and rooted deep.

As the trees grow strong in fertile
soil,
so we mature in the garden of
Love,
nourished by the Word of Life.
For the weeds of fear, the tares
of ignorance,
find no home here; they are
soon cast out.
As each flower in its uniqueness
blesses the garden,
the interconnectedness of all
brings it to fulfillment.
Those whose lives reflect goodness
and integrity,
become mirrors to Love's way.
They are like fragrant blossoms that
bring joy to all around them,
like open invitations for others
to come.
Come! Enter the Garden of Love!

Psalm 126

When the Divine Lover enters the
human heart,
all yearnings are fulfilled!
Then will our mouths ring forth
with laughter, and
our tongues with shouts of joy;

Then will we sing our songs of praise,
    to You, O Beloved of all hearts.
For gladness will radiate out for
        all to see;
        so great is your Presence
            among us.

Restore us to wholeness, O Healer,
        like newborn babes who have
            never strayed from You!
May all who sow in tears
    reap with shouts of joy!
May all who go forth weeping tears
            of repentance, bearing
            seeds of Love,
Come home to You with shouts
        of joy,
        leaving sorrow behind.

Psalm 127

Unless You, O Divine Creator, build
        the house,
    those who build it labor in vain.
Unless You watch over the city,
    the watchers stay awake in vain.
For it is in co-operating with You
            from morn to evening,

Eating the bread of Life and Grace,
 that we rest in peace throughout
  the night.

Reverence the sacred gift of life that
  nourishes all.
Who will grow in wisdom, abandoning
  themselves into the Chalice of Love?
Who will open themselves to the
  imprint of Love's gifts upon
   their heart?
Unless You, O Divine Spirit, make
  your home within us,
  we wander through life in vain.

Psalm 128

Blessed are you who reverence
  the Beloved,
  who walk in Love's way!
You radiate an inner joy
  and peace where'er you go;
  compassion draws you to
   the gates of those in need.

Families and friends gather upon
  your doorstep;
Children run to greet you with
  open arms.

Yes, blessed are you who reverence
the Beloved!

Strangers feel at home in
your presence;
the oppressed are comforted
by your support.
Blessed indeed are you who reverence
the Beloved!
Peace is within you!

Psalm 129

Lift up your hearts to the Most High!
Let the earth ring with songs
of praise!
Be glad O people of the
Light!
Let your life be impregnated by
Love's gifts.
Discover in the Great Silence the
mystery of who you are,
and be true to your Self.
For wherever you dwell,
there is beauty;
Infinite Love is everywhere.
Know that the beauty hidden within
your soul,
is seen by the eyes of
your heart.

Let the still small voice of
        the Beloved
    guide you by day and
    comfort you at night;
Then will you be blessed and,
        in turn,
    you will be blessing to
        the world.

Psalm 130

Out of the depths I cry to You!
    In you Mercy, hear my voice!
May you be attentive to the
    voice of my supplications!

If You should number the times we
    stray from You, O Beloved,
        who could face You?
Yet You are ever-ready to forgive,
    that we might be healed.

I wait for You, my soul waits,
    for in your Love I would live;
My soul awaits the Beloved
    as one awaits the birth
        of a child, or
    as one awaits the fulfillment
        of their destiny.

O sons and daughters of the Light,
  welcome the Heart of your heart!
  Then you will climb the Sacred
   Mountain of Truth;
  You will know mercy and love
   in abundance.
Then will your transgressions be
   forgiven; and you will know
   the Oneness of All

Psalm 131

Most gracious Presence, let me not
  be arrogant,
  nor boast of my virtuous deeds;
Let me not seek fame or set my heart
  on the riches of the world.
Help me to calm and quiet my soul,
  like a child quieted at its
   mother's breast;
  like a child that is quieted,
  be so my soul.

I shall be at peace in You,
  O Breath of my breath,
  from this time forth and
  forevermore.
   Amen.

Psalm 132

Enter into the Silence, into the
        Heart of Truth;
For herein lies the Great Mystery
      where life is ever unfolding;
Herein the Divine Plan is made known,
      the Plan all are invited to serve.
Listen for the Music of the Spheres
      in the resounding Silence of
        the universe.
May balance and harmony be your aim
      as you are drawn into the
        Heart of Love.

Those who follow the way of Love
      with calm and faith-filled
        intent,
Know that all is working toward
        healing and wholeness.
And may the healing power of Love
      lift you from the limitations
        of fear and ignorance
        into the arms of freedom.
May the peace of the Spirit bless
      you, and
      lead you on life's journey.
Be not afraid of the Silence, for
      Wisdom's Voice is heard there!

As you follow the Light, you become
      gentle and kind,
      you come to live in the Light
        and see through Love's eyes.

Children enter the world radiating
             the Spirit—
        learn from them of innocence
             and simplicity;
Learn to co-operate with the
             unseen realms,
        to see beyond the veil.

Wise are those who learn through
             silence;
        learn then to listen well.
For beyond the silence and stillness
             within,
        you will come to know a profound
             and dazzling Silence—
Herein lies the Music of the Spheres,
             the harmony of creation.
Enter into the Sacred Altar within,
        converse with the Beloved in
             sweet communion.
Blessings of the Great Silence be
             with you as
        you help to rebuild the heart of
             the world with love!

Psalm 133

Behold, how good and pleasant
it is
when brothers and sisters
dwell in unity!
It is like vistas seen from
atop a mountain one has
climbed . . .
Or like the stillness of a sunset
after a long day's work.

It is like a shimmering rainbow,
breaking through a
summer rain.
When men and women dwell in
harmony,
the star of Truth appears!

Psalm 134

Come, bask in the Light of Love,
all you who would serve
the Divine Plan!
Lift up your hands to the Holy One,
singing songs of praise!
Bow down and receive blessing from
the Giver of Life!
All praises be to You,
whose Love created heaven
and earth!

Psalm 135

*L*ift up your hearts, all you
who choose the path of Life!
Sing songs of praise to
the Beloved—
To the Holy One, who encompasses
all creation with Love,
to You, who enter all open
hearts!
We raise our voices in praise
to You;
we call upon your Holy Name!
For You call us your friends, and
invite us to commune with
You by day and through
the night.

For great are You, closer than
our very breath.
Through You the world evolves—
in heaven and on earth,
in the heights and in the
depths.
In You and with You do we live
and have our being,
You, who send your Spirit to
dwell in our hearts!

Yes, You are with us in the trials
and temptations of life;
Your mercy and strength uphold us
when fear and injustice
prevail.

You forgive our transgressions,
      our shortcomings and wrongdoings;
You lead us Home when we have
         gone astray, when we have
     chose paths that lead to
        darkness.
You have given us a birthright
         of Love,
    a heritage of Truth.

Your Name endures forever,
      your kindness is imprinted
        for all eternity.
For in your mercy, You reclaim
        the people,
     with steadfast patience
      and compassion.

The nations have chosen material
        idols—
     the lure of silver and gold.
With their mouths they utter
        falsely,
     blind to the people's needs;
Their ears are deaf to the
        cries of the poor,
     they breathe greed and
        spit out arrogance.
Awaken, O people of earth!
      Unbind the fetters of stone
        hearts
     that balance, and harmony
        may be restored!

O nations of earth, bless the
             One Spirit!
    O people of the world,
        gather together in unity!
O children of Light, radiate
             blessings to the universe!
    Surrender yourselves to Love!
Blessed be You, O Beloved,
             Breath of our breath!
    Praises be to your Holy Name!

Psalm 136

O sing praises to the Beloved,
    whose Love sustains us;
Yes, give thanks to the Heart of
    all hearts,
    whose Love sustains us;
And bow down before the Most High,
    whose Love sustains us!

To You, who spoke and Creation
             was founded,
    Your Love sustains us;
To You, who by understanding
             created the heavens,
    Your Love sustains us;
To You, who spread out the earth
             upon the waters,
    Your Love sustains us;

To You, who set the planets upon
their course,
Your Love sustains us;
And the sun to rule over the day,
Your Love sustains us;
The moon and stars to rule over
the night,
Your Love sustains us.

To You, who call us to repentance
and rebirth,
Your Love sustains us;
To You who accompany us as
we face our fears,
Your Love sustains us.
With a strong arm to uphold us,
Your Love sustains us.
To You who liberate us to live
into our birthright,
Your Love sustains us.
Who sends the Counselor to lead
us on paths of peace,
Your Love sustains us.
Who comforts us in times of sorrow
and loneliness,
Your Love sustains us.
To You, who give us a hunger
for prayer,
Your Love sustains us.
And a thirst for You,
Your Love sustains us.
To You, who are quick to forgive
and remember not our sins,
Your Love sustains us.

To You, who instruct us in
                  truth and justice,
            Your Love sustains us.
And in mercy and compassion,
            Your Love sustains us.
To You, who open our hearts to
                  the cry of the poor,
            Your Love sustains us.
You call us to radiate your Love
                  to the world,
            Your Love sustains us.

To You, who remember us when we
            are downtrodden and
                  discouraged,
            Your Love sustains us.
And bring Light into the darkness,
            Your Love sustains us.
To You, who are Loving Companion
                  Presence,
            Your Love sustains us.

O sing praises to the Beloved,
            whose Love sustains us!

Psalm 137

Plunge into the Ocean of Love,
    where heart meets Heart,
Where sorrows are comforted, and
    wounds are mended.
There, melodies of sadness mingle with
    dolphin songs of joy;
Past fears dissolve in deep harmonic
    tones,
    the future—pure mystery.
For eternal moments lived in total
    surrender
    glide smoothly over troubled
    waters.

Hide not from Love, O friends,
    sink not into the sea of despair,
    the mire of hatred.
Awaken, O my heart, that I drown not
    in fear!
Too long have I sailed where'ere
    the winds have blown!
    Drop anchor!
O, Heart of all hearts, set a
    clear course,
    that I might follow!
Guide me to the Promised Shore!

Psalm 138

I give You thanks, O Blessed One,
     with my whole heart;
   before all the people I sing
     your praise;
I was humbled when I came to see
   that You dwell in me, in the
      Sacred Chapel of all souls;
   my gratitude knows no bounds!
For You are the Holy One,
   the Life of our life.
On the day that I called,
     You answered me;
   the strength of my soul
     You increased.

All the leaders of the earth shall
   one day praise You,
When your Spirit Awakens in
     every heart;
And they shall proclaim the new
     dawn of Light and Love.
Great will be the radiation of
     your Glory!
For even as You are the Most High,
   You are Friend to the lowly;
   the arrogant close their hearts
     to your love and guidance.

Though I walk in the midst of trouble,
   You preserve my life;
You are a very Presence as I face
     my fears and doubts;
   Your strength upholds me.

You guide me as I pray to fulfill
       my purpose on earth;
    You do not forsake those who
       call upon You.
    Your steadfast Love and Truth
       endures forever.

Psalm 139

O my Beloved, You have searched me
       and known me!
You know when I sit down and
       when I rise up;
    You discern my innermost thoughts.
You find me on the journey and
       guide my steps;
    You know my strengths and
       my weaknesses.
Even before words rise up in prayer,
    Lo, You have already heard
       my heart call.
You encompass me with love where'er
       I go,
    and your strength is my shield.
Such sensitivity is too wonderful
       for me;
    it is high; boundless gratitude
       is my soul's response.

Where could I go from your Spirit?
Or how could I flee from
your Presence?
If I ascend into heaven, You are there!
If I make my bed in darkness,
You are there!
If I soar on the wings of the morning
or dwell in the deepest parts
of the sea,
Even there your Hand will lead me,
and your Love will embrace me.
If I say, "Let only darkness cover me,
and the light about me be night,"
Even the darkness is not dark to You,
the night dazzles as with the sun;
the darkness is as light with You.

For You formed my inward being,
You knit me together in my
mother's womb.
I praise You, for You are to be
reverenced and adored.
Your mysteries fill me with wonder!
More than I know myself do You know me;
my essence was not hidden from You,
When I was being formed in secret,
intricately fashioned from the
elements of the earth.
Your eyes beheld my unformed substance;
in your records were written
every one of them,
The days that were numbered for me,
when as yet there was none of them.
How precious to me are your creations,
O Blessed One!
How vast is the sum of them!

Who could count your innumerable
gifts and blessings?
At all times, You are with me.

O that You would vanquish my fears,
Beloved;
O that ignorance and suffering
would depart from me—
My ego separates me from true
abandonment,
to surrendering myself into
your Hands!
Yet are these not the very thorns that
focus my thoughts upon You?
Will I always need reminders to
turn my face to You?
I yearn to come to You in love,
to learn of your mercy and wisdom!

Search me, O my Beloved, and know
my heart!
Try me and discern my thoughts!
Help me to face the darkness within me;
enlighten me, that I might radiate
your Love and Light!

Psalm 140

Deliver me, O Giver of Breath and Life,
        from the fears that beset me;
    help me confront the inner shadows
That hold me in bondage, like a prisoner
        who knows not freedom.
They distract me from all that I yearn
        to be,
    and hinder the awakening of
        hidden gifts
    that I long to share with others.

For I desire to be a channel of peace;
    to reflect the beauty of
        Creation!
O, that I might manifest your love
        to all whom I meet,
    and mirror your mercy
        and justice!
Guide me, O Beloved, that I may
        become spiritually mature;
    Love me into new life!

For are we not called to make Love
        conscious in our lives?
    To divinize the earth with
        heavenly splendor?
Reawaken my sense of wonder that
    I may childlike be;
That I might flow in harmony with
        the universe, and
    be a bearer of integrity.

I know that You stand beside those
        who suffer, and

You are the Light of those
imprisoned in darkness.
Surely You will guide us into the
new dawn,
that we may live as co-creators
with You!

❧

Psalm 141

I call to You, O Blessed One,
suffuse me with your Love!
Give ear to my prayer when
I call to You!
May my supplication be heard as I
surrender before You,
as I abandon myself into
your Heart!

Set a guard over my mouth,
O Divine Counselor.
Keep watch over the door
of my lips.
May I speak only what is of good
intent, and
not busy myself with rumor
and gossip;
incline my heart to what is
beneficial and holy.

Lead me to words of wisdom and truth,
    seeds to be planted in my
        heart-soil;
Guide me to times of solitude and silence
        that nurture new growth,
    so my love may ripen into
        abundant fruit.
Cultivate in me a heart great with
        compassion and mercy,
    a peace that radiates out to
        all of Creation.

My inner being yearns for You,
    O Beloved,
        in You do I find refuge and
            strength!
May your Light so shine in me that
    others are attracted to your
        peace and harmony.
In the company of your friends,
    may I, too, walk the pilgrim road
        to wholeness and holiness,
            O Heart of all hearts!

Psalm 142

I call to You from the depths of
        my being,
    with loud voice, I cry out
        to You!

I pour forth my fears before You,
I confess the doubts that I
feel within.
When I am weary and my heart faint,
You are my Rock!

In the paths where I walk, is it
not You
Who knocks at the gate of
my heart?
And are You not the Voice of Mercy,
comforting me in times of
trouble?
Yes, your Presence washes over me,
like the ocean lapping the
shore.

I call to You, O my Beloved;
for You are my refuge,
and in my understanding.
Come to me in the Silence, drop
pearls of wisdom into my heart.

Forgive me for every unkind word
and thought;
Release me from the prison of fear
that I might rejoice and
offer thanksgiving!
Transform my weaknesses into new life,
that I may be a gift of your love
to all I meet.
Amen.

Psalm 143

O Bringer of Joy, Awaken my heart;
pour your love and blessings
through all my being!
Free me from attachments and desire,
that I may become a clear mirror,
reflecting your love to
the world.

For fear has pursued me, it has
crushed my spirit to
the ground;
it has veiled your Light so
that I dwell in darkness.
Therefore, I cry out to You,
O Great Awakener;
Help me to rise once again
like the phoenix of old!
I recall days gone by; I meditate
on all that You have done;
I muse on the Covenant of
your Love.
I open my heart to You;
my soul thirsts for You like
a parched land.

Strength comes with pureness of heart.
Cleanse me anew, O Gentle Healer.
This yearning within my soul is
naught but the inner birthright
to know and live in You.
Let me hear your Voice within the Silence,
for in You I put my trust.

Teach me ways of loving service,
        that I might co-create with You,
           O my Beloved.

Help me to face my fears,
           O Divine Nurturer!
I call on You for healing!
Instruct me in your Divine Precepts,
         cultivate my soul!
Lead me into deep silence and
         solitude,
        let peace become my mantle.

Divine Light shines in those
        whose lives reflect love.
        As the river makes its way to
           the ocean,
        may I surrender to the flow
          of new life!
Then will I trust that all is
        working together toward the
          wholeness of humanity.
        Then will I help to rebuild the
          soul of the world with Love!

Psalm 144

Blessed are You, O Radiant One,
    You, who are hidden within
        our hearts,
    even as we are hidden within
        your Heart!
You invite us to participate in
    the Divine Unfoldment,
As we Awaken from our long sleep
    and give birth to creativity.

Open us that we might recognize the
        divine in every person,
    and become sensitive to all we
        meet along the path.
For You are the Breathing Life of all,
    the infinite and eternal within
        our hearts.

Evoke the Child in our souls,
    that purity and grace might
        flourish!
Inflame us with compassion so
    we nurture ourselves and others
        with healing and forgiveness!
Empower us with wisdom and knowledge,
    that we might bring forth
        the Divine Plan!
And let us recognize the Truth
    that clear vision might unfold.

Let us sing a new song to You,
    O Beloved;
        with drums and flutes let us
        express our joy!

You who are Divine Love, receive
       our devotion,
   that we may walk in beauty.
May our heart's ears heed well
     the Divine Word written on
        every heart,
     that integrity and justice may
        dwell within us.

Let each one be receptive to the
        Spirit that inspires,
    allowing our will to respond
      with action;
And may all judgments and denials
       be released,
    that our souls are freed to
       to serve the Light with joy!
Thus will we recognize oneness with
     The Divine Spark dwelling
       within our hearts,
    fanning it to illuminate the way.
Gratitude and inner peace will abide in
      every tranquil soul,
    blessing the universe that
      lovingly cares for us.

Psalm 145

My souls yearns for You,
      Eternal Flame of Love,
    longing to reconnect to
      the Great Mystery!
Every day I will bless You as
    I follow the Voice of Truth.
Great are You, who call us to
      childlike wonder,
    to the healing balm of forgiveness.

Each generation must learn anew
      the efficacy of silence,
    the wisdom of turning inward,
That your Light might be their
      guide to holiness,
    and your Love nurture them
      toward wholeness.
Yet, many there are who turn from
      You in fear,
    denying their birthright.
Their denials will lead them further
      into alienation;
    loneliness will companion them.

The Beloved is gracious and merciful,
    allowing every soul free will to
      follow the ego's illusions or
        to choose Life.
Gratitude and quiet joy overflow
    as I recall the abundant
      blessings of your grace!

Lift up your hearts, all you
    who choose the path of Life!
      My heart is lifted up!

"Do you not know that your whole
being is
encompassed by My Love?
I am the infinite and the eternal
within your soul;
O, that I might make Myself
known to you!
Choose Love that you might overcome
oppression and blind obedience
to false idols!"

"Divine Light shines in those
who live in Love.
I shall uphold all who are
burdened with fear,
and raise up all who call to Me.
The time is nigh for you to choose,
for great is the new dawn
that fast approaches;
I call each of you to open your
inner ears, to
see with spiritual eyes,
And to trust that even amidst the
outward chaos,
all is working toward the
wholeness of humanity."

O, Heart of my heart, envelop me!
I know You are near to all
who call upon You.
Bring to my recollection all that
I have denied,
that I might be accepting
and free
To help rebuild the soul of the world
with radical trust, love,
and wonder!

When I speak, let it be of
                blessing and gratitude;
        let your glory within me shine
                out to the world!

Psalm 146

Praise be to You!
Praise the Beloved, O my soul!
I will praise You with all
                my being;
I will sing joyfully and with
                thanksgiving
        to You, Heart of my heart!

Put not your trust in riches,
        in illusionary things that
                fade away.
For when our day comes to depart
                this world,
        at that very time, we carry
                only the love
                imprinted upon our soul.

Blessed are those whose strength is
                in the Beloved,
        whose trust is in You,
                O Divine Lover,

Who gave birth to the universe—
      the heavens, earth, and sea—
          and all that is within them.
You are ever-faithful, bringing
        balance and harmony to earth,
     nourishment to body and soul.

You free us from the bonds
      of fear;
     You give insight to those
       who would see.

You lift up the faint-hearted,
      giving succor to those who weep.
You watch over those on journey,
      sending guides and angels
        to lead the way;
O, that we might become beacons
      of light
     to those in darkness.

May You, who live forever in
       our hearts,
     loose the fetters of fear
      that bind us,
That we might praise You always
     with free and joyful song!
      May it be so!

Psalm 147

Praise the Beloved, Heart of all hearts!
We are blessed as we sing praises
    to the Beloved;
For as we give ourselves to love,
    so we receive Love.
The Beloved abides in our heart,
    in every open heart that
        welcomes Love.

Through Love we are sent to the
        brokenhearted,
    a mutual balm to the soul.
We seek out the downtrodden,
    those without shelter or food,
    recognizing our own poverty
        with them.
Those in prison also await willing
        hearts to visit them,
    that forgiveness might free
        all from bondage.

Sing to the Beloved with thanksgiving;
    mingle with the melodies
        of the spheres!
Awaken to your inheritance in all
        the universe!
    For you belong to heaven,
    to the stars and galaxies.
You come also from the earth, from
        mineral and plant,
    pure water courses through your veins.
Every creature—those that swim and fly
        and walk on land—
    knows you as of old;

And each human—in body or in spirit—
        welcomes you in the heart-song
                of Love, where we know
        we are all One Being.

Praise the Beloved, Life of all life!
        Invite Love into your heart!
For Divine Love gives strength to
                the weak, with
        courage to face their fears.

Divine Love brings peace to the
                heart, peace
        that is beyond our knowledge.
Divine Love cuts through the ignorance
        that fosters greed and arrogance,
        humbling and breaking open
                the heart.
Divine Love severs the veil that
        separates realms of the
                profane and sacred;
Holiness radiates through all
        touched by Divine Love,
        a refining Fire!
Wisdom flows from the Heart
                of Divine Love
        to all receptive hearts nurtured
                in the Silence.
Yes, the Divine Word is written
        on every heart-scroll,
        a guide to pilgrims on the way.
May everyone awaken to Divine Love,
        that peace and integrity and
                assurance
        may be born again in every land.
O my soul, praise the Beloved!

Psalm 148

Praise the Blessed One!
Give praise from the heavens,
    and from all ends of
        the earth!
Give praise all you angels,
    angels of earth and of heaven!

Give praise sun and moon,
    give praise, all you shining stars!
Give praise, all universes,
    the whole cosmos of Creation!

Praise the Blessed One!
    For through Love all was created
And firmly fixed for ever and ever;
    Yes, the pattern of creation
        was established.

Give praise to the Beloved,
    all the earth,
    all that swim in the deep,
And all the winged ones in the air!

Give praise all mountains and hills,
    all trees and all minerals!
Give praise all four-legged
    and all that creep on the ground!

Leaders of the nations and all peoples,
    young and old,
Give praise! Unite together in all
    your diversity,
    that peace and harmony might
    flourish on earth!

Let all people praise the Beloved,
who is exalted in heaven and
on earth;
whose glory is above heaven
and earth.

For all are called to be friends,
companions to the true Friend,
giving their lives joyfully as
co-creators and people
of peace!
Praises be to the Blessed One,
the very Breath of our breath,
the very Heart of our heart!

Psalm 149

Praise the Beloved!
Sing a joy-filled song praising
the Blessed One among
the people!
Be glad in the Creator,
rejoice in Love Divine!

Praise the Divine Lover with dancing,
with melodies and voice!
For the Beloved dwells within,
journeying with us through
all our lives,

Leading us in truth and love.
The humble are adorned with honor;
   the faithful exult in glory,
      singing for You with
      thankful hearts!
With truth on our tongues,
   with gratitude as our friend,
We are in harmony with the universe,
   as we hold hands with
      all the people.
The chains of oppression are broken,
   the fetters of injustice unbound.
The realm of Peace and Love shall reign!
   Glory abides with those who are
      faith-filled.
Praise the Beloved!
   All people on earth, welcome
      Love's Companioning Presence
        who abides in your hearts!

Psalm 150

*P*raise the Beloved!
Praises be to You in earth's sanctuary;
   praises be to You in the mighty
      firmament!
Praise the mighty works of Love;
Praise the glory and extol the
   greatness of Love Divine!

Give praise with trumpets;
    give praise with lute and harp!
Give praise with timbrel and dance;
    give praise with strings and reed!
Give praise with booming drums;
    give praise with crashing cymbals!
Let everything that breathes
    praise the Beloved with their lives!
       May it be so now
          and forever!
       Amen.

❀

Half of the profits from these verses will be donated to Friends of Silence, a nonprofit endeavor to facilitate others in reverencing Silence, prayer, and contemplation and to encourage the life-giving empowerment that derives from the Silence. For further information, write to:

Friends of Silence
Center For Peace and Prayer
11 Cardiff Lane
Hannibal, Missouri 63401

Lumen Christi . . . Holy Wisdom
Journey to Awakening

This inspiring book contains admonitions, challenges, and encouragements for the reader to move up another step on the spiritual ladder. In short, these are spiritual self-help exercises for personal improvement. The gentle hints and suggestions come in the form of meditations and brief contemplative insights. This is not what was often called over the centuries a book about "the way of perfection"—not even of "the little way" of perfection. This is a book that will help the hesitant inquirer who is making the first gestures toward a vaguely glimpsed, but longed-for, inner contentment.

"Nan Merrill is the Rumi of the Christian faith! Her intimate heart-knowledge of God as the Beloved quietly radiates from each page of her poetry, awakening that same confidence in the reader. To spend time with her is more than just a pleasure; it is a blessing!"

—The Rev. Cynthia Bourgeault, Ph.D., author of
Love Is Stronger than Death